D0840976

MEETUP LEADER:

How to Run a Successful

and Profitable

Meetup Group

Gary Zenker

Copyright 2014 Gary Zenker.
All rights reserved.

The Meetup name and logo and any other related trademarks are property of Meetup Inc. Screen captures are Copyright 2014 Meetup. They are used as examples only with no infringement intent.

I have no official association with Meetup to advertise or promote their services.

All information in this book is based on my personal experience with Meetup and running events and meetings across the country. It also includes references to others who have been generous enough to share their perspectives and experiences with me.

Other company names are or may be copyright or trademark of their respective companies.

ISBN printed version:
9781941028087

TABLE OF CONTENTS

INTRODUCTION

Leadership is a special trait and one not everyone possesses. If you've chosen to start a group from scratch or run an existing group of any sort, you're at least part leader whether or not you started out thinking that you were. Congratulations! You are one of the few.

There are many joys and challenges in being the leader of a group. Watching your group members learn and grow is a tremendous thrill. Seeing achievements that are the direct result of your contribution as a leader is extremely gratifying. Done right, a leader serves as both a figurehead in the spotlight and a reflector of that same spotlight onto others. Knowing when to be which is a very special skill and an important part of your leadership role.

The very things that make the experience so gratifying are also the source of your challenges. Managing people can be especially challenging, as they hold personal goals that sometimes conflict with the group's goals. Some individuals will be extremely self-focused and disruptive no matter how carefully you communicate the values of the group. You, as a leader, have the responsibility for getting your group to the end goal. So, managing the people component of the group is especially important.

Your reasons for leading a group may be business motivated. Many business people use Meetup.com groups as a feeder for different business lines or leads. There's certainly nothing wrong with that, as people will attend (or not attend) based on the value THEY RECEIVE from the group. Running these types of groups requires the same leadership skills as managing any other groups in life: credibility, organization, knowledge and talent.

LEADERS VS. MANAGERS

In life, some people think of themselves as leaders but in reality are actually managers. Leaders show people a path and then get the group members to 'ride the bus' to the end destination. Managers tend to focus on the projects as opposed to the people. And although they both may be trying to get to the same place in the end, the paths and efforts of the two are often very different.

A co-worker once told me of the existence of a *responsibility tax*. That tax falls on those who are truly responsible for the burden of making things work. Other people may or may not work, or they may or may not be fully engaged. It's the leader who takes on the responsibility of getting the work done, engaging and re-engaging the group members as necessary.

So the fact that you care enough to read someone else's thoughts on running a better Meetup.com group qualifies you as one of these "responsible" people. Congratulations, because it also means that YOU will have the ability to make great things happen, and the wisdom to consider different ways of achieving your group's goals. I hope that by reading this book, you'll learn some new things, apply them, and then find your own wisdom to pass onto others -- because that's what a leader does.

THE REAL PURPOSE OF THIS BOOK

This book is intended to support your efforts in running a group, combining knowledge of the Meetup system with experience in managing projects and groups of people in a variety of situations.

As of the time this book was written, the computer screen captures and processes for making things happen within the Meetup system were accurate. But we all know that applications change often. If by the time you read this, a few of the examples and how-to's are out-of-date.

AN APOLOGY OF SORTS

I realize that throughout this book there are many examples from the groups I personally run and a few from other Meetup groups I have attended. It isn't meant to seem self-serving, but I am very familiar with these examples and the foundations on which they rest. There are good lessons to be learned from them, both things to do and avoid. With this book to guide you, you will be able to duplicate the successes and avoid the mistakes that my friends and I have made running our own groups!

AND A REQUEST

You have had your own experience, successes and even a few less-than successful-experiences in running your own groups. I encourage you to share your tips, tricks and advice so that we can both help others. Send your emails to garyzenker@gmail.com. I can incorporate them into the next edition of this book. I'll be happy to acknowledge you when your information and feedback is used.

Thanks and best wishes for your great success.

MEETUP.COM AS A GROUP MEETING TOOL

WHAT MEETUP.COM IS

Meetup.com is part community and part meeting-group resource; it works well in both areas. Used correctly, it can be a constant feed for new members and a valuable tool to save you time and energy in managing your event coordination efforts. I highly recommend it highly for managing your groups.

If you are reading this prior to establishing your first Meetup.com group, here are a few important details you should know:

- Meetup.com is a social media platform/application that is free for individuals to join.
- Meetup.com charges organizers for the privilege of running an online Meet Up group site. You can pay monthly at a rate of $19.99/month or pay for six months at a time for $72.00. The latter plan gives the organizer the ability to run up to three separate groups. So unless you are really unsure that the group will last four months, the six month option is a much better buy.
- Meetup.com offers both computer desktop access through their website and mobile optimized access through a specific app.
- Individuals who join the Meetup.com community enter key phrases that describe their interests. Meetup.com can then direct individuals information on groups related to their interests. Individuals themselves can search the community for groups that match their interests.
- Groups establish their own criteria for online joining (immediate access or requesting permission before being approved), types and amounts of fees, etc.
- Groups can assign different leadership responsibilities and restrict different kinds of site access based on the roles people

are assigned; the organizer can restrict specific data or group functions as he or she wishes.

- Meetup integrates monetization of the group. Use of their payment system requires a nominal fee for each payment processed.

Meet Up offers an unmatched online resource for common-interest groups built specifically around the needs of the organizers and the desires of individuals.

AND WHAT MEETUP.COM IS NOT

Although it offers many things, Meetup.com is not a replacement for your in-person meetings. While the web presence and a larger Meetup community offer a lot of capabilities, it is not designed to be your total group presence. Unlike Facebook, designed in many ways to be a community complete unto itself, Meetup.com is designed to work best in conjunction with live meetings.

Whether in-person live meetings are held once a week, once a month or four times a year is up to you to decide. It should be whatever benefits *your* group members and leverages your resources. But Meetup.com does not truly integrate any form of actual meetings. That's all left to you as the group leader.

And Meetup does not replace a full function website covering other aspects of your group. While it is flexible and even allows you to create custom web pages, it's no match for a fully functional web site. You may need one of those, too.

INCORPORATING GROUP MANAGEMENT SKILLS

To run a successful group, you need to have more than just good tools, even a tool as good as Meetup.com. You also need to *know how to use them* AND *incorporate group management skills*. That's where this book and its examples will help you leverage the MeetUp.com application and community to achieve your goals.

This book offers examples primarily focused around three groups:

The Main Line Writers Group has been in existence since January 2009, growing each year in membership and involvement while other local writers groups have stagnated and shut down. The group began its life as a Meetup group and has continued that way ever since. It is one of the most successful writers groups in its area.

The Brandywine Valley Writers Group began life in 2003 and grew organically before joining the Meetup community in August 2010. It strategically followed the success of The Main Line Writers Group in using the community to drive new member interest and manage the responsibilities of the group. Meetup.com is now considered core to the group communications and group management efforts.

The Wilmington Writers Group started as a test to gauge interest for a parallel writers group in a new geographic area in December 2013. It hosted over twenty people at its first meeting and consistently has had reservations for fifteen or more members for every meeting since. Like most groups, it needs a bit of time to establish a base core in the early months of operation and continue to expand.

Reference (sometimes by name and sometimes not) is also made to a number of other Meetup community groups including: a network of career groups, business networking groups, other writing groups from the region, and a couple of others assorted groups I have personally attended. These help round out the examples and offer a wider perspective on effective and less effective group meeting characteristics.

A BLUEPRINT FOR MEETING SUCCESS

FOCUS ON MEMBERS' NEEDS AND ORGANIZATION

Each example group's success results from two factors: *focusing on the needs of the members* and *staying organized*. Those sound like two simple and easy to follow concepts; in truth, they are the most difficult and challenging elements of managing any group.

That's because people managing a group, project or business often lapse into focusing on their own needs or those that they *think* people *should* have. The common result is that people and companies succeed in spite of their own actions until...something more focused on the members or customer comes along. Then, *suddenly*, people defect and the organization can't quite figure out what happened. Those in charge make up excuses, blame people who are no longer there (or even some who remain), and maybe even fire someone.

By that time, it's too late; the people are gone and they have to go out and get new customers to replace the ones that they lost. It is significantly more difficult and costly to attract new people than to keep the ones you already have.

So how exactly does that apply to you as the leader of a new or existing Meetup group? Pretty directly, actually. If you are just starting a group, your ability to get people to actually show up and then keep showing up is directly related to whether you can *focus on their needs* as opposed to what you think their needs are or, worse yet, by focusing on your own needs.

And if you are already running a group, you need to ensure that people keep coming back or you will constantly be trying to replace them with new people. If you are indeed doing that, you should really be asking yourself "What am I doing wrong that people don't want to stay in the group?"

That is a crucial question. If that is your pattern, it likely will continue to be your pattern going forward, even with new people joining the group. The easiest way to spot that error in focus is to look at any written words or record yourself speaking. If your sentences start with "I" or "we", it's a dead giveaway that your focus is internal. In fact, if you have more than one or two "I" or "we" in a given paragraph, odds are good that your focus is off your target market. And that is the most serious problem you can have.

HOW THE MAIN LINE WRITERS AND OTHER GROUPS MAINTAIN FOCUS ON MEMBER NEEDS

So how did I manage this better in our groups? *Focusing on the needs of the group* comes directly from my marketing background. People have a lot of different reasons for running a group, any group where people come together. There's almost always an ego component involved. And that ego can often cause leaders to select paths that are in direct contrast to the group members' needs. A good leader acknowledges their own ego up front, and takes steps to ensure that it doesn't compromise core goals through actions incongruent with the group members' interests.

Those steps include listening closely to a tight core group who provide honest and direct feedback. It also includes my asking the questions such as "Did I talk too much during the last introduction?" and "What do other people think about the group?" to nearly anyone who is willing to answer. First timers are often asked what they think about the group, as well. And when we hear criticism, we ask the questions "Is it valid?" and "What should we do about that?"

Let's acknowledge this fact up front: not every group is meant for every person. And not every criticism is valid. Even so, I start out listening to every single comment as though it is. The trick is to try not to look at criticisms as a sign of failure, but rather as a way to make the group better and stronger. That will help save you from taking any suggestions as being criticisms toward your leadership.

WHAT ORGANIZATION REALLY MEANS

Organization can mean different things to different people. Most important about the concept is what results from it: the group meeting accomplishes what you set out to accomplish and it runs smoothly. To my groups, that means an agenda covered successfully. It means that all the things we need to run the meeting efficiently are present. And while we are flexible in what we cover, reacting to a need on-the-spot can be a positive thing, we sometimes move specific discussions that come up to a later time to ensure that we don't go off on tangents and miss the meetings' core goals and objectives. It's all about active management of the meeting and respect for the members.

Staying organized doesn't mean I am always perfect. But it means we know what we have to do when, and on which resources we can absolutely depend. It means prioritizing actions based on what will have the most meaningful impact on and to the group, whatever surprises we encounter or tangents we may travel.

Those two elements aren't the only reasons for any group's success, but not following them is generally all you need for a total failure. So it's important to get those two right, first and always. Everything else flows from them, one way or another.

YOU DON'T NEED PERFECT KNOWLEDGE OR SKILL
TO BE A GOOD LEADER

Leaders aren't always the most knowledgeable on a particular topic, nor necessarily the best at whatever they do. What leaders do have is the special ability to bring together people and the things they want or need, in a way that resolves issues, achieves goals and gains the respect of others.

I joke openly in the writers groups I lead that I am the least well-read and least prolific *creative* writer in the group. For my own work, I spend a great deal of time writing business plans, ad copy, web content and that kind of material...just not so much creative fiction and such, which is a primary focus of the group.

Following one session where I made this admission to the group during its introduction, one newbie came up to me. He hesitated before finally asking "If you are the least well-read and least prolific writer in the group, what qualifies YOU to run this group?"

"A good question," I smiled and immediately answered "because I know how to run a group efficiently, find and provide excellent content, and create an environment of learning and sharing. Because I'm a leader who listens to what the other members believe that a writing group should include and needs to accomplish, and deliver on it."

More important than what I believe is *what the group believes*. They see me as the leader. They look to me for continued leadership. They follow my lead, which in reality is *a careful reflection of what they want*. I offer guidance to prevent straying off course. The group could take many directions, some of which would be dead ends. As leader, I need to be able to see further out than they can, and help them reach the goals and avoid the dead-end paths in the process.

My role as the leader of the Main Line Writers Group and the Wilmington Writers Group began as the direct result of founding the group. My *continued* role as leader is the result of being the person most committed to it and all of its goals, in terms of time and resources allocated to the group. It turns out that no one within each group has shown the desire to run the group. Even with its current success and after repeated requests as to whether anyone would like to manage the Main Line Writers Group, no one has stepped forward.

The Brandywine Writers Group has had the same leaders (sometimes exchanging the specific positions) for several years running. On the surface, it sounds like fun to be leader. And while most people are very grateful to the people who run the groups, they are just not interested ininvesting the work it would take to be part of running the group.

In my groups, I have a team of people that help me manage a variety of functions. It is a great team of very special people (see the acknowledgements at the back of this book). Some of the members have agreed to take on very specific and defined roles within the group. They, too, are leaders, even if they don't necessarily view themselves as such.

In the Main Line Writers Group, we have a talented person who runs all the critique meetings. I have an individual who acts as treasurer and collects the membership money and distribution of receipts. We had a person take on the project management associated with the book that the group produced in late 2013. And we had a dedicated person who took on the role of arranging the launch party for the group's book launch. Not one of them wants to run the overall group, but each accepted a clearly defined and more limited responsibility readily.

The Brandywine Valley Writers Group has six specific leadership roles within the group including treasurer, web site management, one dedicated specifically to program management. Meetings run smoothly, are well organized and accomplish specific goals because the people involved are happy with well-defined roles that limit their overall time involvement.

And the good news is that the bulk of the members are very comfortable showing up for whatever programming is planned, the result of well-structured, strongly focused meetings.

Contrast this to the free-to-attend *Philadelphia Area Career Success Groups* Meetup. Professional career counselors created the groups as weekly offshoots of their monthly networking and meeting group, for the benefit of job seekers who wished to get together on a more frequent and informal basis (and maybe to serve as leads for their pay services). The leader is whichever attendee accepts ownership (the career counselors do not attend, run or offer content for the meetings), which changes as people find jobs and no longer attend.

The challenge with the groups is knowledge and expertise: as job seekers, they aren't necessarily qualified on the topic nor are they necessarily experienced leaders. They share opinions more than facts and while they attempt to help each other, the advice they offer is mixed in terms of accuracy. There is no legacy for group leadership over time and outside prep efforts for the groups are minimal. There are no guide documents beyond what someone in the group may have created for him or herself. With a change in leadership often comes a change in structure.

The informality may appear to be a plus at first, but the lack of structure is a definite minus. These groups have a tough time meeting the stated goal to "share best practices about job hunting and career development...and "give each other...discipline and energize their career-building campaign." Many of those who attended later dropped out, finding that it wasn't worth their time. THAT makes a huge statement about the groups' leadership.

This very clear contrast shows why people come to the writers group meetings for inspiration and the career group meetings out of desperation. And that makes for very different results in attendance and ratings of the groups.

LEADER COMMITMENT AND GOAL FOCUS

It sounds like a big "duh," but by involving the membership with well-defined and focused roles, you can accomplish a number of things:

- Drive more active involvement of individual group members
- Collect opinions on topics that concern them
- Create a greater sense of pride and connection with the group
- Extend your own network of connections
- Reduce the amount of work and volume of details which you have to personally handle.
- **Expand the overall capacity and offerings from the group**

That last point is emphasized purposefully because that is the ultimate goal for the groups that I manage. My goal isn't really to minimize my own work (although some days, that can seem more important to me than others). But with my groups' best interests in mind, the goal of expanding capacity and offerings drives most of my actions as a leader. What we can offer that people want and how far can we develop that offering without reducing our quality are important factors in my decisions regarding the group.

PROGRAMING AS AN ELEMENT OF GROUP LEADERSHIP

An important element in leading your group is your programming management. The first thing most people need to learn is how to give up some of the control they have and which control to retain.

In addition to possibly being the least prolific creative fiction writer in the group, it should be noted that I also lack the connections (or at least used to lack the connections) to other writing professionals that many of our group members possess. Now you REALLY wonder how and why I can run not one but two writers group, right?

A perfect way to compensate for that weakness is to make strong connections with the people within the group who *are* connected. They already know lots of great writers who are also great presenters. So I involve them and get their opinions on who we should invite as presenters and guest speakers.

In the beginning, I only invited presenters whom I had personally seen speak. That was fine as I was learning my group as individuals. But it quickly became overwhelming with the time commitment involved and my own limitations. I needed to trust my members. An amazing thing happened when I did that. They came through!

When shifting the control from myself to them, I offered specific criteria for selecting a speaker: the presenter needed to be engaging and skilled at their topic. The only other requirement was that they needed to have personally seen the person make a presentation. That presenter could be a relative, a friend, a neighbor, a professional acquaintance or even someone they barely knew; but someone needed to have *personally seen* the individual present

Some of our guest speakers were referred from individuals who had never published a piece and some from individuals who have been published hundreds of times. But members had to have attended enough of our meetings to have seen a variety of presenters and understand the quality we were seeking. The only time I erroneously accepted a referral from a newcomer was also the only time that the guest speaker cancelled his presentation without notice and the member only came twice before not attending any more. Lesson relearned.

Why not present on all of the topics yourself? After all, you are the leader.

There are lots of ways to answer this. Here are just a few:

- Because your group may deserve to receive more knowledge or experience than you have on a topic.
- Because you don't want to appear a "know-it-all" (even if you are).
- Because it's tiring doing all of the work
- Because doing that makes you blind to the full needs of the group.
- Because you will appear to be a stronger leader by involving others in the content presentations.
- Because you can lead just as well or better from a sitting position within the group.

As leader of groups, I limit my own presentations to the "housekeeping" portion of the session (which is often a shared responsibility as I call on others to cover the topics) and seldom present any other content for the group.

That isn't because I can't make the presentations or that I am uncomfortable presenting in front of a group. My career required presentations to the board members of banks and credit unions; sales presentations to company owners and groups of entrepreneurs; and training to hundreds of marketers from professional groups. I love to present and I love to teach.

And I don't avoid presenting because I don't know anything on the topics. When we talk about marketing or humor or a dozen other writing-related topics, I could easily give the presentation or lead the group in discussion spontaneously.

I purposely choose not to present because my primary goal isn't to show the group how smart I am, or to reinforce by own self esteem by being the teacher most of the time.

As an aside, I didn't take the group title President; I am the Co-Founder and Lead Facilitiator because President sounded pretentious and ego-laden to me. With a title of President, I was concerned that I might forget my purpose and goals: to lead a group that educates, shares and engages the membership.

I get my body and my ego *out of the way* wherever I can, so the people who ARE presenting can do it to the best of their abilities. The credit for the quality of the group comes from all of the talented and sharing members we have. Their involvement is critical for a long-term successful group.

My real job is to make certain that the environment supports their involvement and take away any stumbling block. The goal is to shine the spotlight on others and make them feel good about what they are accomplishing, and give them resources within the group to turn to for answers.

In doing this, I have been rewarded with a group that shares those philosophies and embodies them in all of our programs and with all of the new people who come to check us out. That's what gives the group depth and power. That's why the group keeps growing. And for me, as a leader, that's what I find is the real payoff.

FIRST STEPS: DEFINE YOUR GROUP SUCCESS MEASURES UP FRONT

With any endeavor, success can be defined in a number of different ways, depending on who is doing the defining. Someone else's measures of success may not be what you consider success. That's why it is so important to define success up front. Part of the process is to determine how YOU define success... and continually re-evaluate it throughout your group's existence.

A leader with a particular goal might define it one way; members may define it differently. In fact, individual members are likely to define success differently from each other. Some show up to learn something; others may come to meet new friends; for some the goal may be just to get out of the house and still others may be there to sell something to other members. There are some who attend just to show off their own skills.

Your goal as a leader is not necessarily to enable all people to meet all of their goals. We all know that's nearly impossible to do. Strive to pick some goals that make you happy and that fulfill the needs of a group. Depending on the goals you select and their importance to attendees, you can run a group that has ongoing attendance and satisfied members.

Notice that I didn't say you have to run a large group, or an extremely profitable group. Those measures MIGHT be your measures of success. But those and other measurements depend on a number of factors, including the competition for your members' time and money, their real need for your offering, and the base value proposition it offers.

SOME EXAMPLES IN DEFINING (OR NOT DEFINING) SUCCESS

One factor people typically use in measuring success is the *number of members*. But it's also a factor that may take you down the wrong path, because raw numbers alone are generally not a true sign of success.

Use the Main Line Writers Group as an example. It's great to see that the group has 370+ individuals who have joined the Main Line Writers Meetup Group online. If certainly sounds impressive on the surface.

You might also be interested in the fact that over half the people who have signed up for the group have *never* attended even one in-person meeting. Okay, that starts to sound a little less impressive. That's pretty typical of Meetup groups where signing up for the group itself is free and you don't eventually force people out of the group for non-attendance.

What I do know through experience is that 26-40 people are coming to each in-person meeting. Is that considered a success or failure with over 370 members? And how does that compare to when the group started with 21 members and 12 showed up? More successful or less successful? Once again, the answer depends on how you want to define success. Large online membership does not necessarily equate to large in-person participation.

My group goal is *not* to have the largest number of online Meetup members, but to have a highly engaged group who attend to learn and lend their experience and knowledge to others.

That said, we have defined success for the Main Line Writers Group in this way:

- Attendance of at least 20 people who are actively engaged during the meeting.
- Meetings where people treat each other with respect regardless of their writing level or publishing success.
- The percentage of return attendees is at least 50%.

- The level of "welcomeness" new attendees feel on their first meeting.
- High quality meetings as rated by the attending members.

I personally set a goal that attendees should find the meetings to be the best time that they have invested in their own education and skills development or self-motivation efforts for writing for that month.

So given what I just said, is there a reason you might still consider raw number of people in your online Meetup an important part of your success? Sure, because when you have a large number of people who have opted in to your online group, you also then have a large network of people who have opted in to hear your message. It may take months or years before they eventually attend a meeting. They may actively pass the announcements onto their friends or their friends may passively discover your group. I can't think of a way that having a large numbers of followers will hurt you – well, unless they all show up at once unexpectedly.

YOUR DEFINITIONS OF SUCCESS

So how should YOU define success? I can't answer that for you. What I can do is list a number of measures that you may want to consider in constructing your own answer to the question:

- Number of people signed up for the group online.
- Average number of members attending.
- Average number of times attendees actually attend.
- Number of paid memberships.
- Reviews and feedback on quality of meetings both at the meetings and afterwards.
- Percentage of members that return more than two times.
- Percentage of new people who attend each meeting.
- Attendees as a percentage of those signed up to online MeetUp.

- Involvement level of the people attending meetings.

Of course, the list of possibilities is endless. Just consider this: you can't be focused on all of them simultaneously. You will have to choose one or a few from the list of possibilities. The ones you do choose will focus your efforts, and your efforts will attract some people but not others. In fact, your focus efforts may *actually alienate* some people. While that may not be on purpose and it may not be your goal, it's likely to happen. If you have chosen your goals correctly, you should be okay with that.

EXAMPLES OF SUCCESS DEFINITIONS

As a Writers Group, we hold the goal of wanting people to learn and share with each other. The group offers programming (presentations) related in some way to writing or publishing six times a year and critique (people bring their works in progress for feedback) the other six. I have some people who show up every meeting. Those people come either because they want to learn and improve their skills in a variety of areas or because of the relationships they have formed with other members.

Some members attend critique sessions only. My programming alienates them from half of the meetings because critique is the only part of the program we offer that they feel is worthwhile to attend. But because the group goal involves helping writers from a variety of aspects, I accept that result in attendance. It's okay for them only to come to the critique meetings.

Likewise, different topics attract different people. When writers come to present, attendance is often dependent on the program topic. While some writers believe that a presentation by writers of any genre have value, others who attend have no interest in areas other than their own specialty. So attendance changes when I have a thriller writer or a romance writer. Sometimes I get people coming for just the one program, like when I offer a presentation from a literary agent (someone who represents writers to book publishers). And while I wish I could get those one-timers to come on a frequent basis, I stay true to the group goal of providing a wide range of information and topics for writers. Changing content to please some would discourage others, and changing too often would confuse members as to what the group's purpose really is.

In the end, it's up to you to set the overall structure and tone for the group based on its goals.

GOAL SETTING EXERCISE

Now it's time for you to put your group goals down in writing.

Complete this form by thinking about the goals that you would like the group to achieve and the resulting type or characteristics of members that those goals are likely to attract. Don't worry about a priority order for them just yet: leave that column blank. Just get them down on paper. Write down any goals you have or want to have. Start with the Group Goal column:

GROUP GOAL	PERSON LIKELY TO BE ATTRACTED (Characteristics, Types, Interests)	PRIORITY

If you prefer to perform this goal-setting exercise using a computer spreadsheet, you can download this and other book spreadsheets at www.ZenkerMarketing.com/downloads

NOW, approach the question from the opposite view. Think about the type of person or characteristics of members that you would like to attract. Extrapolate what group goals would most attract that type of person. Again, don't worry about a priority order just yet; leave that column blank. Start by completing the PERSON column.

GROUP GOAL	PERSON LIKELY TO BE ATTRACTED (Characteristics, Types, Interests)	PRIORITY

Compare the two lists. They are likely to have overlap but perhaps be expressed using different words with the same overall meaning.

Use the form below to consolidate the two lists.

GROUP GOAL	PERSON LIKELY TO BE ATTRACTED (Characteristics, Types, Interests)	PRIORITY

Now you need to assign a priority to your stated goals. It is highly unlikely that you will be able to accomplish everything on the list: some of your goals may naturally conflict with each other. You have to pick one or just a few that will serve as the guidepost(s) for your group to focus all of your efforts.

SELECTING BETWEEN COMPETING GOALS

Many people have trouble selecting between competing goals, so here's a strategy to help you. Start by dividing the items into A, B and C groups. You can have as many A's as you like. The A's should be the ones you think are non-negotiable. When you have done this, go over them again and affirm your decision.

Move the B's and C's out of sight but don't destroy them. The fact that they are B's and C's does not mean they are unimportant…it just means that they won't be our primary focus. We'll come back to them shortly. Focus on the A's. The goal is to place the A's in an order of relative importance. To do this, use A1, A2, A3 etc. as ratings. Compare the first one to the second one. Which is more important? Take that one and compare it to the next unrated A. Take the winner of those two and compare it to the next until you have gone through the entire list.

Some people do this easily just using the grid provided. Many people find it beneficial to place each on a three by five card and ordering them on a table. Do whatever works best for you. In the end, you should end up with a list of A prioritized goals. Fill out a clean chart with the goals listed in priority order, most to least important.

GROUP GOAL	PERSON LIKELY TO BE ATTRACTED (Characteristics, Types, Interests)	PRIORITY

Add back the B and C goals to the bottom of the list. Effortlessly, you've created your priority lists!

To begin with, you will set out to achieve as many of these goals as possible. If there's a conflict between two, allow right of way to the higher rated goal without second thought or additional angst.

SUMMARIZE GROUP GOALS: A COMMITMENT STATEMENT

Organizations and groups often create a Mission Statement to help communicate their values and goals to staff and clients alike. Conceptually, it is a great idea to help guide an organization. There's just one small problem with it: it starts out completely wrong as a message for clients.

A Mission Statement is written from the perspective of the organization. "We will..." or "We are" (replacing we with the name of the organization) is typically how these things begin. In corporate America, they are often followed by some unrealistic or unbelievable statements, like "We are the market leader..." blah blah blah. For other organizations, they focus on the things that they want others to believe that they will do: "We will provide support for..." or "We will enable clients to maximize their..." And that's exactly where it all goes wrong.

That's because *a Mission Statement is all about the organization itself,* written in terms of the organization and what they do, what they strive to do or what they hope to convince others that they do. If you really want to be a member or customer-driven organization focused on your group members' needs, you *never* show them a Mission Statement.

Commitment statements voice the benefits which the member, client or customer receives *from their standpoint.* As such, they start with phrases like "Members will receive..." or "Group members get..." That difference in focus changes everything, not only in the way people read it but how the organization views what they do and what their focus is. Try it. Construct your own Commitment statement using the information you compiled in the Goal Setting Exercise.

You can use one of the following to start writing your Commitment:

- Members of the _____ Group will...
- _____ Group members will...

Use one, two or three of your A priorities to communicate what members will receive and what values the group prioritizes. Be concise and clear in your wording.

Some are a few examples of what group members might receive:

- ...opportunities to network with peers and professionals
- ...educational seminars covering topics related to....
- ...participation in activities related to...

Write a couple of versions and put them away for a day. Then pull them out and review them. Read them to someone who is not involved with the development of the group and ask them to explain, in their own words, what you are saying.

Then make it your cornerstone for your group implementation.

YOUR MEETUP GROUP DESCRIPTION

Your Meetup group description (ABOUT US) is one of the first things people will check out to determine whether your group is a fit for them, so it holds great importance. Spend some quality time working on the text and ensuring that it is in line with your group goals.

What to write

Write for readers (even if it isn't a writers group). Your first instinct may be to keep your text brief, because people just don't read. That belief isn't true at all. The real truth is that *people don't read what bores or disinterests them*. They read plenty of what does interest them or what they feel they need to know. The New York Times Best Seller List and authors like JK Rowling and Stephen King can attest to the fact that people do indeed read long passages of text. *As long as it is relevant to their needs and holds their interest.*

That means you need to keep your text focused on what people want to know.

And for goodness sake, write an outline **first**. Your fourth grade teacher (and every teacher you had since then) was right: doing an outline up front improves most written work. It keeps your writing on track for communication and minimizes the amount of time you have to work on your text.

How to write it

How you say it is every bit as important as what you say. Your entire concept can be right, but the words you choose and the structure you use to present those words can make people want to read it or stop after just a few words.

Make it personable. MeetUp has an informal feel about it to begin with, so use that to your advantage. Make your description friendly and personal; make the reader feel as though the message was written just for her (or him).

Keep your sentences and paragraphs short. Lengthy paragraphs of long sentences are difficult to read…studies show this is true, especially on a screen. Keep your sentences shorter but keep a good rhythm and flow, which often means alternating the length of sentences. Using all short sentences makes your writing feel choppy and rushed; using all long sentences makes it feel like a Faulkner novel. This, by the way, holds true on all areas of copy for the web, not just the group description.

Keep your paragraphs to 5 lines or less wherever possible. You'll increase your readership and they are more likely to follow any instructions you offer. That's because the eye can easily (and automatically) skip over long paragraphs of type.

Use the right words

Marketers spend years learning and relearning how to make people respond and what triggers their responses. Ironically, as fads come and go, the words that form the core of responsive copy don't change all that much. That's because even while things like technology and style change all around us, people's core needs stay fairly constant.

You may not be a writer by profession, but if you want to write copy that makes people join your group, you need to understand the reasons, as well. You probably think that FREE is the most common activating word. Think again.

YOU is the most powerful word that you can use. For the very reason you went through the previous exercises and identified the most important points to your audience, the focus should be on the group member(s). A 2007 study showed brain activation when hearing one's own and other names. If you don't want to take my word for it, take a look at the study for yourself. http://www.ncbi.nlm.nih.gov/pmc/articles/PMC1647299/

Nevertheless, **FREE** is no slouch as a motivator and is generally considered the second most powerful motivating word. But because it is so over-used, many copywriters have switched to using the word *complimentary* to express the same thought. Unfortunately, with five times as many syllables, the latter takes longer to say or read and then to mentally digest. On the surface, it appears to be classier and isn't as overused as FREE. But free still says it quickly and efficiently, even if everyone doesn't quite believe it.

BECAUSE holds strong power in influencing actions. Robert Cialdini's classic book *Influence* tested the use of words and phrases in the context of people in a hurry to use an in-office copy machine. Give people a reason for your need and they respond more positively to your request. And while giving weak reasoning still performs better than giving no reasoning at all, but giving better reasoning offers better results.

FAST, INSTANT, IMMEDIATE, QUICKLY and other words that express time value work incredibly well to influence actions. Since faster is almost always better than slower (I'll leave your imagination to the times when it isn't), and sooner is in nearly every case more desirable than later, it's easy to see why these words hold such weight in creating human response.

NEW remains one of the top five influencers, as well. New is often viewed as better (than not new) because of its association with being up-to-date. Classic sometimes holds the advantage on being better built, but that's only if you're old enough to have a history or hold that belief. Many of the people we communicate with don't have that history or hold that belief.

It's important to remember that you have to use this information contextually. Forcing the words or concepts where they don't belong results in your text doing the exact opposite of what you want it to do: it becomes unbelievable and influences people's actions in the opposite direction.

How to present it (and all text content)

Perhaps you can remember back to the days when a parent or some other figure of authority told you that "you can't judge a book by its cover." And the primary reason they need to tell you that is because we do, very often, judge a book by its cover.

First impressions are very often influenced by the physical appearance of an item. We can use that to our advantage, especially on the web where we have so many options to control the way things appear. Long unbroken passages of type are hard to read because of their lack of visual call-outs. The eye blurs all of it together and goes looking for something, *anything* that is more interesting. When that happens, odds are good that the person never goes back to the text, or when he does, repeats the same dismissive actions.

We have access to a great number of tools we can use to help visually reinforce the message the text is giving, IF we understand how the eye works and reads, and how the tools can be best used to help guide the reader through the text we offer.

Use of text formatting options. You can incorporate all the standard formatting options including bold and color type, etc. Here are options you have and a few quick facts about their use to make your formatting support more effective communications.

> **Create short, bold subheads**. They can be used on their own line or as the beginning of a paragraph, every three or four paragraphs at the very least. If appropriate, do it for every paragraph. It may seem overdone but you are more likely to get your message across better, especially if you have written that

bolded phrase correctly. See the examples through this book on how to do it and how well it works.

Use italics sparingly. Italics type is hard to read and decreases reading comprehension significantly, especially for long passages of type. Use it as emphasis for just a few consecutive words within paragraphs. *Never* use italics for emphasis on entire paragraphs.

Use bold, color, capital letters and indents in a uniform way. These are your tools of communication, which helps make your points better. You need to incorporate them all. The bold in the default MeetUp text doesn't always look especially bold, so using color and all caps helps to differentiate certain phrases and words.

Use plenty of blank lines. Blank lines help chunk text into logical segments and aid the eye (and brain) to avoid being overwhelmed by a sea of grey.

Use underlines to separate elements, not to emphasize text. Underline was used historically to emphasize text because typewriters didn't have the capability of incorporating bold and/or italics. Underlining is a poor vehicle for word or phrase emphasis. Use bold, color and capitals for that function, not underlining. Use underlining to focus a header or separate blocks of text.

Manage the lengths of the lines of text. Lines of text that are too long or too short make it difficult to read. The appropriate length of a line varies with the size of the type you use, so stating it in optimal numbers of words per line is easiest. Five to fifteen words is a good length to use, depending on the context of the medium.

Ragged right type improves legibility (in general). That's because, once again, long blocks of type are easy for people to skip over when you have long horizontal lines of text. Blocks of type that are full justified (aligned evenly on both the left and right sides) confuse the eye…it's harder to go from the right edge back to the next line on the left side. The eye gets confused.

It may *look neater* to have justification on both the left and right sides, but it is harder to read. Consider which is more important to your goal achievement.

Indent bullets under the text it follows. A personal pet peeve. Bullets need to left align but should be slightly indented to make them easy to read. Bullets offer a list format, which is harder to read if they left align with the text above it. Bulleted entries should be short, just a line or two, or you ruin their effectiveness as a visual reading tool.

And add a little extra space (leading) between the last line of the bullet and the beginning of the next one.

- Adding space between the last line of the bullet
- And the first line of the next bullet
- Makes it much easier to read them as separate items

- Adding space between the last line of the bullet

- And the first line of the next bullet

- Makes it much easier to read them as separate items

Does it all seem like a lot to keep in mind? Once you start doing it the right way, it becomes second nature. Until then, use the above as a checklist and make adjustments accordingly.

Remember that these guidelines work anywhere you have text in Meetup or on your web site. They apply to fliers and other printed materials, as well. Use them and I guarantee that your communications will be clearer and more understandable to everyone who reads your words. And as a marketing guy who studied the effects of how type is used, I know that's a fact.

DEVELOP YOUR LEADER PROFILE

It may seem out of place to break into our discussion on the group by focusing on your own profile, but consider this: next to the group description, people will look to the leader's profile to get a sense of the leader and of the value of the group.

The **Your Profile** pull-down menu on the far right of the group menu bar provides access to your information.

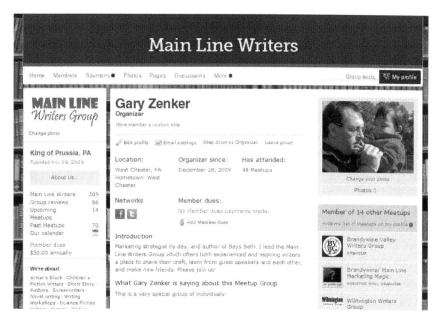

Your introduction allows just 250 characters. That's enough to tell a good story IF you write carefully and concisely. In fact, the limitation is excellent as it forces you to focus on the most important elements and eliminate irrelevant text. This information is not supposed to be a comprehensive resume or your life story. It covers your role as leader of the group, so keep it relevant to that function. Use it to establish your credibility. Again, make it warm and friendly.

Because of the structure of Meetup and the groups, giving a first person description and using the word 'I' **once** is a great way to make the greeting feel personal. But using the word "I" more than once runs the risk of being too self-focused (and honestly, just looks amateurish).

You can make a different and additional statement about the group itself the same way you can comment on any Meetup Group. In that mode, you should not use the word 'I' at all. Your narrative should be all about the group without qualifying statements such as "I believe" or any "I" phrase. Start the comment with "The Group" or "The {group name} is ..."

In addition to holding the title Organizer, you can also give yourself another title using about 50 characters. Go ahead and do it. It helps establish your credibility up front, especially if you perform multiple roles within the group (as most leaders do). Titles you might consider are: Founder, President, Facilitator, Chair, Program Director, etc.

Your photo says a lot about you, so use a good one. While some Meetup users sometimes omit a photo for a variety of reasons, as a group leader it's important that **you** use one. You need to give people every reason to trust you. Hiding your face from potential members accomplishes just the opposite.

The type of photo you want to use should relate to the type of group you lead. Is your Meetup a group of runners? Instead of a face shot, maybe a head and torso running photo is more interesting. Or any photo that relates to the activity of the group. But of course, at the very least, something that shows your face.

Here's an example of using your group context to help in selecting your photo. In place of a standard portrait, I consciously selected one that I liked with my (then) two year old son. Unprofessional? Unrelated to writing? Well, consider what it does show. It does show my face clearly and it does present an image of me as a person (and hopefully as a leader). Caring. Sensitive. Nurturing. Those characteristics seem to be a good match for someone leading a writers group, whose members may be introverts, shy to mix and do much of their work in solitude. When they come to a group, they are looking for people who share their passion, a place where they feel safe to talk about their interests in a deeper way and to connect with others. Given all that, I believe that my photo reflects a leader for the environment they seek and with whom they feel that they could connect. But if I were running a business networking group, this is definitely NOT the photo I would use.

Criteria to consider for your Leader Profile photo

What picture should YOU choose for YOUR profile? The one that is the right mix of the characteristics you want to present. Here are a few thoughts to consider when selecting that profile photo:

- Make sure people can see ALL of your face. TAKE OFF the sunglasses unless your group is a Meetup for sunglass wearers.
- Smile for goodness sake. Nobody wants to join a group where people are unhappy, especially the organizer.
- Keep your background either neutral or relevant to the group you run. A picture with a McDonalds sign in the background shows you don't understand the importance of details or how they affect perceptions. It can distract from your main goal.
- Use a sharp, clear image.
- Have someone actually take the photo for you. Lose the amateur selfie taken in the car or in the mirror; you are the leader of a group. Look like one, behave like one.
- Have a fear of double chins? No problem. Instead of having the camera facing you straight on, have your photographer a step or two above you. It works wonders.
- Look at other photos and model yours after the ones you like best. Angled shots are more interesting than straight on face shots.
- The profile photo crops to very specific dimensions, and the size used differs depending on where it appears.

- If you want people to see what you look like, a basic head and neck shot is best.
  - When listed as an organizer, it appears approximately 159 x 154 pixels.
  - When it appears next to a comment you make, it appears approximately 80 x 77 pixels.
- To make certain your photo looks great, crop the photo in advance to the nearly square specifications of Meetup. Otherwise, Meetup will do its own cropping and may cut off part of your face (see example below)

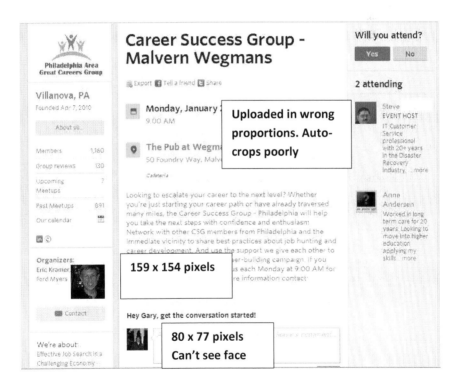

Account Settings

Your Email Settings screen will help you with your ongoing group management as leader. The automatic notifications send messages to your designated email account at a frequency you prefer.

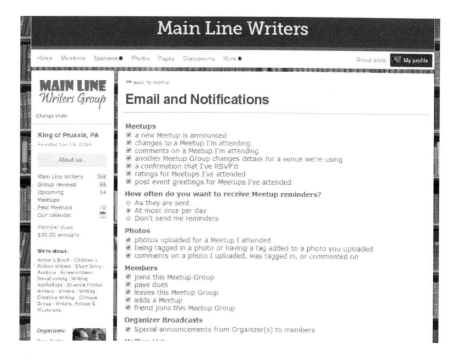

Activity within the group depends on the number of members in your group and other factors: it isn't generally overwhelming. I personally like to see things (like meeting RSVPs) as they occur, so I've opted for emails on any activities.

You can select once daily or weekly, but if you select these less frequent updates, you run the risk of appearing unresponsive to people asking questions or needing more information. Consider that even if you get notices as they are posted, you can respond to them as you want. Ultimately, the choice is yours in how you monitor and manage the group activity. Meetup gives you a lot of options from which to select.

You can change your settings at any time, so set them one way and then see how it works for you. Then make changes as necessary.

MAKING PEOPLE FEEL WELCOMED

Much of my groups' success is based around one simple but important underlying philosophy: everyone should feel welcomed in the group from the moment they arrive.

Please don't underestimate how important this is to the success of your group, or any organization or business for that matter. We all have been in situations where we didn't feel comfortable or welcomed.In cases where there is no requirement that forces us back, like a paycheck, there are generally many other options to replace it.

A year and a half before starting The Main Line Writers Group, I joined a different writers group that was very cliquish. It shouldn't have come as a surprise...they already knew each other and I was the newcomer. While I wasn't rebuffed, I also wasn't welcomed and felt alone most of the night. I almost didn't go back.

It took a few meetings to get a feeling of fitting in. When other people came for their first meeting, it was easy to look across the table and see (and feel) their isolation. Unless they were somehow engaged, and quickly, it was clear (to me) that they would never reyurn. So I made it my responsibility to start conversations with them and welcome them in a way I hadn't been.

They came to the group looking for a connection but were often overwhelmed or too shy to move beyond showing up. And the existing writers didn't do the kind of outreach they could have. That's probably not a surprise: most writers are introverts. And most people spend time talking with those who they are most comfortable with - people they already know.

Eventually, I became a part of that group's core - showing up consistently does that. I built relationships. It could also be partly due to the fact that other members who were previously part of the core left. An opening for me! Today, six years later, some people believe it is my group (not exclusively mine, just mine) because of the strong social role I held and hold.

So when I began my group, the Main Line Writers Group, I told my story to everyone there and that I wanted all of them to find our group a safe and welcoming place. I still tell my story to new members on a regular basis.

And I model the welcoming behavior at all times. I try to greet new members personally in the beginning of the meeting or catch them at the end and thank them for coming, and offer a wish that they return.

Most have very positive things to say. Some come regularly, some irregularly and some never return. But I can say with total confidence and without hesitation that the reason they fail to return is never because they didn't feel welcomed or didn't connect with someone that evening. It may be too far a drive or a bad night of the week. They may not appreciate the multi-genre programming. But they all feel welcomed because that was and is the number one priority on the Main Line Writers Group goal list, ahead of education and everything else. Fortunately, it is congruent with all of the other group goals.

The group is our home and we have invited people in. I model the principle that we treat them as if we had invited someone in our home: greet them as they enter; address them by name; engage them in conversation; encourage their involvement at whatever writing level they are, and tell them that we hope they will return for the next get-together.

MAKE THEM FEEL WELCOME FROM THE MOMENT THEY JOIN

A great opportunity to make people feel welcome is when the person first joins your Meetup Group *online*. A couple of kind words can make a huge difference in how fast that person attends an in-person meeting.

After all, joining the on-line group is easy and free, and requires almost no effort. Showing up to an actual meeting in person requires a bit more effort and is the first point of disconnect. Making a connection online leads a lot of people to make the decision to actually show up, which in turn is the only way people will feel a real connection to your group.

Spread the welcoming responsibilities. Both online and at the meetings, there are strong reasons to select specific people to serve as ambassadors for the group.

First, you can't be everywhere at once. As your group grows, you may be able to send everyone new a fast note online but you won't be able to talk to everyone at the meetings. In an effort to leave no visitor behind, you will need help.

Second, you don't *want* to be the only one doing the greeting. Having others serve that function gives them purpose, engages them in a deeper way, and offers multiple points of welcome for the newcomers. Newcomer relationships start right there and then!

Get multiple people involved with the welcoming and the newcomers will take on the role for others, as well.

SCHEDULING YOUR MEETINGS

SCHEDULING MEETINGS THAT ARE EASIER TO REMEMBER

Setting dates that are easy to remember makes a huge difference in getting people to actually attend on an ongoing basis. *Consistency* and *predictability* is important.

The Main Line Writers Group has chosen to make the meetings on the third Wednesday of the month. The Brandywine Valley Writers Group meetings are always on the third Tuesday of the month. The Wilmington Writers Group is the second Monday of the month.

Great Careers Groups hold theirs weekly. Monday meetings are in one city, Tuesday meetings in a different city. Wednesday meetings...well, you get the idea.

Scheduling meetings in this way is easy. No one needs a calendar in front of him to tell people when the meetings will be held...it's *always* the third Wednesday of the month. Sure, we know and announce the actual date as well. But you want to know when the October meeting is being held? Even without a calendar, you can tell people the answer they need without hesitation.

People are accustomed to this type of scheduling and it fits better into their existing schedules. If someone is taking a class, for example, it's generally at the same time on Wednesdays or Tuesdays or whatever.

There's a definite cost advantage for marketing the group and its meetings, as well. When you make banners or posters, they can be used ongoing without replacements or sloppy changes. I can use that same poster for years, announcing Meetings on the third Wednesday of the month.

Ideal meeting dates. The ideal dates for your group depends on your group members and the nature of your Meetup. As examples:

- If your group consists primarily of housewives with school-age children, you would probably be wise to consider weekdays during the day before school lets out. You might also find that some week-nights or even weekends might work as they want to get away from the daily responsibilities and socialize with others not related to children.
- If your group is a group for aspiring writers, weekday meets won't work. They are probably working other jobs which would make day time meetings impossible. Meetings starting at 6:30 or 7:00 pm on a weeknight might be ideal. Or it could be a weekend morning or afternoon.
- A career group might seem ideal at 7:30 am so people can attend early and go off to work or start their day. But if the other spouse is working and needs to leave for work early in the morning, and they have kids, you may well eliminate the possibility of some people attending. A later start might make a huge difference in attendance.

If you pick days and times where you make people choose between your meeting and something else they typically *like* to do, you better offer damn good value or prepare for sporadic attendance. For example, unless your group is entertainment focused, a Friday evening business networking meeting seems doomed to failure.

And remember that attending your Meetup may not be free of cost to attend, even if you don't charge a membership or meeting fee. Baby sitters can make a meeting cost $20 or more to attend. It's not your worry but scheduling time where it doesn't cost your target group extra or make them miss paying work is something you should consider.

So know your audience and their needs. Understand what their typical requirements are. It will help guide your date and time selections.

CHANGING MEETING DATES - AVOID IT

Your meeting dates should be as close to unchangeable as you can possibly make them. It's not that I recommend that you be inflexible in everything – flexibility is a strong measure of success. But stable and predictable meeting dates set a strong foundation for your group. If you are continually changing your meeting dates, you've chosen the wrong meeting date mechanism to start.

It takes extraordinary circumstances to force our groups to change a meeting date from our regular schedule. If our meeting falls the day before Thanksgiving or Christmas, we change it out of necessity, *but only after surveying the group about whether it actually is a problem.*

And I believe I've changed the Main Line Writers Group meeting date just twice in over five years, due to my personal schedule and the fact that I was key to the presentation being given that month. In general, the meeting goes on whether I can be there or not. That makes an important statement to everyone in the group. You can rely on the group and the meetings go on, even if the lead facilitator is absent.

When we did feel the need to change the date, we announced it well in advance and we did it often. In each announcement, we make it clear that it was a one-time change to the schedule, and that meetings would revert to our third Wednesday of the month schedule with the next meeting, reinforcing the regular meeting date.

In fact, I consider the regular meeting day a more important constant than the location of the meeting, which I am also loathe to change (see Selecting A Meetup Location later in the book) once a group has been established.

You could try picking an arbitrary day like the 15th, but people and other organizations generally arrange their schedules by days of the week, so having it a Wednesday one month and a Friday the next and a Tuesday on the following month is often confusing and difficult. **And moving from a weekday to a weekend is often a recipe for disaster.**

CANCELLING MEETING DATES

Sometimes circumstances give you no alternative. Your meeting place may be closed due to a power outage or some disaster beyond their control. The weather may make traveling dangerous. Or maybe the meeting place has double booked the meeting room. There come times when you are just going to need to cancel your meeting. How you do it and how you communicate it can make a huge difference to your membership.

No one should be left guessing whether you are or are not holding the meeting, and they should all know how they will be informed in advance.

Please take a lesson from our excellent local school system on cancelling school due to weather or other circumstances. They have phone numbers and email for the parents, and make decisions no later than 5 am for the day's school schedule. Notice often comes as early as the evening prior. That notice comes to our telephones through pre-recorded messages and through emails. As parents, we know *how* we will be informed and *by what time* the decision will be made.

As a Meetup leader, I watch the weather 48 hours in advance and try to make conservative decisions giving enough advance notice that everyone will know of changes *before they would head out to the meeting*. No one should ever brave the elements and find that the meeting was cancelled only *after* they arrive at the meeting place.

So in the event we believe the group needs to cancel a meeting, we do it in the morning of the day on which our evening meeting is scheduled. It's the respectful thing to do, and we receive compliments on the way that we handle the communications.

We use the Meetup email system for notifications. Although we have email addresses for some members, we assume that if they can get messages about the meetings through the Meetup system, they can get the cancellation notices that way, as well. We also post cancellations on the group website whenever possible.

SELECTING YOUR MEETUP LOCATION

Setting down some roots. Like date setting, location setting is important. Consistency improves attendance. Holding the meeting in the same place every time may seem a little monotonous...until you consider the benefits.

1) ***As a leader, you know what to expect.*** You eliminate surprises on your part by knowing the room acoustics, the room shape and size, the physical limitations, etc. Familiarity means that you won't spend your first thirty minutes panicking and attempting to fix something that could ruin the effectiveness of your meeting that you couldn't or even should have predicted.

2) ***Your host location gets to know you and your group.*** Your host is one of your most valuable allies in making your meeting a success. They know what they have hidden in a back closet that you may be able to use. They know how their own equipment works and how to rearrange the room to hold more people, or how to make the room look full with fewer people.

   If they are serving food, they've done it often enough to (hopefully) know the actions that will create the least disruption to your meeting. Having you back repeatedly makes you more valuable to them, as well.

   The Main Line Writers Group meeting place, Michael's Restaurant in King of Prussia, Pennsylvania, really prides themselves in their efficiency. To help us, they give us the same waitress *every time*. She was great from minute one BUT got even better after just a few meetings and learning our rhythms.

   Members of our group arrive at different times and separate checks are a necessity. Our group members often move around during the meeting to form sub-groups. That makes us one of the restaurant's most challenging groups to serve. Places like this make it easier to run meetings from a leader's standpoint.

3) ***Your attendees know where they are going.*** Keeping the same location means that your group members will gain a better understanding of how long it takes to travel to your meeting and how traffic may affect their travel times.

This is particularly important for attendees. As an example, following the first and only location move for our group just 15 minutes away, group attendance changed dramatically.

Some people were already traveling a long distance; the extra travel time made the meetings unattractive for them. It is also true that we gained an influx of new people for whom it was now more, rather than less, convenient to attend.

For those who are attending, there's also a comfort to them in familiar surroundings. Sure, new can be fun, but it's also disorienting. For a food tasting group or maybe a travel group, movement between hosting restaurants can be a benefit or even a core attraction for the group. Depending on the group, it can be annoying.

If food is being served and attendees are required to buy their meal, changing locations can without warning radically change their cost to attend a meeting. Surprises of that sort are seldom tolerated well and result in increased dissatisfaction levels. That can create sudden and unexplained changes in involvement and attitudes at the meetings.

Changing locations can also affect start times for your group meetings. If people can't accurately estimate travel time to get to the new location or what kind of traffic they might encounter, they arrive late. It means that your meeting starts may be delayed as you wait for stragglers and push end-times later. Your meetings may have to go much later than planned, or end before you have achieved your meeting goals.

If you want a stable membership that keeps returning to your meetings, make it easier on them and settle on a single location for your Meetup.

FREE IS SOMETIMES WORTH WHAT IT COST YOU....NOTHING

A free place to meet seems very attractive...right up until you realize what often comes along with the deal: excessive noise and a lack of privacy. I've attended Meetup meetings in a variety of locations. Some have been held at local supermarkets that have a great food court within them and we were easily able to move tables together to manage our entire group. As a bonus, people only had to buy food if they wanted to do so.

But the ceilings were high, the radio blared in the background and the overall acoustics were terrible. The result was that people sitting just four seats away from the person speaking couldn't hear what was being said. Not the most effective meeting results. It affects the entire meeting dynamics negatively. But hey, it's free, right???

Paneras and Starbucks are also popular locations because the space is free, they don't monitor food purchases and offer free WIFI. But again, your group and the topics are on public display; the background noise is uncontrollable; you can't always move tables into a reasonable configuration; and they really were never designed for your group needs.

Even the general dining areas of restaurants can pose challenges. We also held meetings in a nice chain restaurant on a Tuesday evening, a typical slower traffic day. The area was free as long as we bought our meals. But the wait staff frequently forgot our request to seat other patrons as far away as possible (and it was impossible to accommodate us on busier traffic days). The music was always turned up and, again, you couldn't easily hear the speaker from four seats away.

Any of these locations may work great for your group, depending on the size of the group, the nature of your meetings and the group's meeting needs. Or you may find that you need something better to keep the group meetings effective and on track.

FINDING A BETTER LOCATION (everyone likes an upgrade)

You could spend dozens of hours driving up and down area roads and stopping in every hotel and restaurant, looking for room availability and pricing. I know...I have. It's a long and tedious process. Save that as a last resort.

First, use Meetup.com to check out all of the Meetup groups held in your area and check the locations of THEIR meetings. Most of the time, there will be not only details on the locations but people will also rate the locations. You can find out quickly places you would never know are available, and hopefully avoid wasting a lot of time. If you have questions, start by contacting the Meetup leaders. They know how hard it is to find a great place and will often make other suggestions that were wrong for their group but could be perfect for yours.

Some restaurants offer a private room. Our room has a twenty person minimum but it also comes complete with an audio visual system which we use three to four times a year. You might also consider asking about a fixed meal where the restaurant prepares a couple of choices in chaffing dishes served buffet style or sandwich trays for a flat per-person price. If it doesn't lower the cost of the meal, it at least standardizes it for all of the members.

Remember that although the restaurant has the room, you hold the economic power of money and meals sold if you get big groups. Don't be afraid to negotiate with them in a respectful way.

OTHER POSSIBLE MEETING LOCATIONS

There are many locations other than restaurants that can serve as meeting places. How well they will work for your group is a function of your group needs and the locations' characteristics. Consider your group's needs in the following areas: privacy, lack of external distraction, hours of access, protection from the weather. Then consider some of the following potential meeting places and how they may match your needs.

Hotels. Most hotels have meeting rooms available but that is typically part of their core business offering, so most of them are too expensive for small and limited income groups. During my inquiries, I found prices range from $150-$350 for a single meeting.

Schools, firehalls and churches. Local schools, universities or satellite campuses may have rooms they are willing to loan or rent out. I've personally attended meetings in Fire Halls (the local Fire Department's building) and libraries. A local assisted living facility was offering free meeting space in one of their community rooms in exchange for the exposure it gave in the community. Churches often make rooms available to the community depending on the meeting topics. Sport centers and gyms may have rooms available, as well. Each of these options will have different limitations on food, hours available and such, so you need to evaluate them for their cost versus the other limitations that come with their use.

Your own group members may be able to offer you special access because of their relationship with the space owner. Don't forget to explore these possibilities within your own membership.

Member homes. For some smaller groups, meeting in member homes may be a desirable option with maximum flexibility. No fee, no arbitrary closing time, and food flexibility including covered dish participation. Just remember that you are inviting strangers into a home.

Local businesses and public areas. Depending on the group, you may find that a local business can be your best host, especially as they relate to your group topic. A sewing club might meet at a Joann's Fabrics. A craft-related group might find that the meeting room at Michael's is ideal. Dog owners could meet at a public park. A book club might meet at a local book store or library. Not every business has a private rooms, but then again, not all groups require one.

Whatever location you choose, if your meeting space doesn't support your meeting needs for privacy, communication, time available, etc, then your members will stop attending. Creative thinking is sometimes necessary to find the best mix of meeting place characteristics to meet your goals and your budget.

THE FOOD BEING SERVED CAN/WILL MAKE A DIFFERENCE

If food is a part of the option or requirement of your meeting space, you need to give it some thought. Bad or mediocre food may not ruin your entire meeting, but it won't make things any easier for you, either.

The type of food served can affect your meeting, as well. Full meal restaurants involve multiple courses...and with that comes multiple interruptions. In fact, if your group numbers twenty or thirty, it can feel like a single ongoing interruption. Our first event at a steak restaurant was a disaster despite the group being located in a private room. Too many courses, too many interruptions.

The ordering and food delivery of sandwiches and similar foods generally makes for less waitress interaction and fewer interruptions overall.

IF FOOD IS THE FOCUS OF THE MEETING

In some cases, food isn't just an option, it's vitally important or the main focus of the meeting. For dating meetups or gourmet groups, you are going to want to focus on locations where the food is excellent. For these groups, it may also be desirable to move locations for each meeting.

You may not get the kind of feedback you need from checking the location reviews in other Meetup groups. Supplement that information with the opinions of members who have already been there for other meals and seek out unbiased restaurant reviews.

FOOD SERVICE – THE 'S' WORD (Service)

Bad food can leave people with a bad taste in their mouths (literally and figuratively); but lousy service can destroy your meeting faster and much more efficiently.

The goal of your meeting should be to have the attendees focused on the meeting-related events, which may include a presenter. At any type of restaurant, loud talking and disruptive wait staff can distract not only the person they are serving but everyone in the surrounding area. And while you would expect that restaurants and wait staff are experienced and conscious of leaving a light footprint during your meeting, that isn't always the case. Often, showing personality and being conspicuously present is how wait staff generate larger tips. It is up to you and your attendees to help them become better at serving you.

One of my groups learned this lesson the hard way from a restaurant with supposedly experienced staff. Here are some of the proactive steps you can take to guarantee smoother and less disruptive service:

- **Meet before-hand with the restaurant manager**. Explain your specific needs and how the meeting will run. If you want service throughout the meeting, tell him. If not, make that clear as well.

- **Meet with the service staff ahead of time** with or without the manager. Explain your needs to them directly. You would be surprised how many times your instructions go unforwarded through a variety of circumstances.

- **Recap your needs with the restaurant prior to the start of each meeting.** Realize that your wait staff may change from meeting to meeting. If you have special or unusual needs, the staff won't necessarily remember them or even have been told about them. They are not mind readers. Clear communication on your part will drive better results.

- **Review the positives and the problem areas with the restaurant manager immediately after the close of the meeting**. Use the sandwich approach in communication: challenges that need to be addressed between a positive beginning and a positive summary. Start with an overall positive statement to make the manager feel that you appreciate the efforts being made. Explain what didn't work and *why you need it*...it will help the manager help you to craft a solution. Then conclude with how happy you are in the location.

- **Establish a relationship with your server directly,** especially if they help you on an ongoing basis. Most food servers want to do a great job and work hard to get things right. They are people and will respond to positive comments and your respect.

- **Let the small stuff slide**. Nothing will be perfect. Don't ruin a generally good performance by focusing on insignificant flaws. Yes, the details are important. One of those important details is your ability to recognize the effort your server(s) put into doing the job correctly.

- **Request a change of food servers if necessary**. Some people won't learn or will take too long to catch on to your needs. You are responsible for the restaurant having a block of business; you are the single point person for interface between your group needs and the location. You should feel comfortable asking for a change if that's what you determine is necessary.

Here are some of the problems many groups that hold their meetings in restaurants have and some solutions you may find useful:

Challenge	Solution
Each individual needs a separate check	Arrange ahead of time for separate checks to be issued
Attendees move around during the meeting and the waitress may forget whose meal and bill was whose	Name cards members can carry with them if they move within the room.
Loud chatter during the meeting between waitress and attendee	Specifically remind both members and wait staff to whisper during the meeting to show respect for the presenter
Multi-course meals create increased traffic	Request that all courses for an individual be brought at the same time
Complicated meals create confusion and a lot of waitress/attendee interaction	Simplify the menu by only offering a subset of the menu for the meeting. If you limit to a handful of choices, you can use color chips to indicate which meal people select and they leave the chips on the table.
Waitress is nowhere to be found when you are ready to end the meeting	Have waitress bring the check before or with the meal; in advance, set a specific time for the wait staff to collect payment.

Remember that although you have a justified expectation to have good food and service (which you and your group are paying for), you (collectively) also have the responsibility to be good guests, as well.

- If the location requires that your attendees purchase a meal, make certain that they know that up front in your Meetup group description and every meeting announcement, and then remind them *before the meeting begins*. It seems that at every meeting, my group has at least one person who appeared surprised when I mention it or thinks that the rule doesn't apply to them, despite the information being written in every meeting description.
- Remind your attendees to take care of the wait staff and ask the staff after everyone has left whether your members did indeed take care of them. To the wait staff, your group is a single entity and you are its representative. You don't want bad service for the whole group the next time you meet because the waitress got stiffed on her tip by one or two members.
- Take the time to thank the manager after every meeting. You don't know what kind of accommodations they may be making to ensure your group is serviced. Yes, it is their job and yes, you are giving them profitable business. Still, everyone likes to be appreciated and hear that they did a good job. The great managers will be right there afterwards asking how things went. Whether they do that or not, be the great guest anyway.
- Recognize the wait staff in front of the group. That 20 seconds you spend doing it will mean a lot to them...because most leaders will never think of doing it.

Remember, if you aren't a good guest, that ideal location can decide not to invite you back despite the profit you earn them for the session.

HOURS AND PARKING

Two important factors in selecting a location include the hours of operation and parking availability.

The official hours of your Meetup and the length of time people actually stay for it may be very different. You want to try to accommodate members who want to stay longer than the scheduled meeting if possible.

The Main Line Writers Group meeting officially begins at 7 pm. Because it is held on a weeknight, people often come to attend straight from work. Some arrive as early as 6 pm to order their meal prior to the meeting start. And although we typically conclude the Writers Group meeting by 9 pm, we do have people who stay and talk until the restaurant closes at 11 pm. Starting earlier is not a possibility because of the number who can't arrive until 7 pm, so offering the extended hours is important. Try to find a location that is flexible enough that you can encourage your members to interact and not have to rush out the door at the end of the official meeting time.

Parking is also an important consideration. If it's too difficult to find a parking spot, or if parking is overly expensive, that can drastically affect attendance. Keep in mind what the *total cost of attendance* is for your members and make it as easy as possible for them to say 'yes' to join your meetings.

MANAGING YOUR GROUP MEETINGS

UNDERSTAND AND MANAGE ATTENDANCE

Tracking attendance plays an important role in managing the success of your group. Having a good estimate of attendance for your meeting, even as little as a few hours in advance, can be the difference between calm success and all-out panic.

Encourage use of the Meetup.com RSVP system.

Meetup has provided you with the ultimate planning tool with their RSVP system integrated into your membership records. You can announce your meetings as far in advance as you like, and members can indicate their attendance in advance and change their attendance status *at any time.* If they use it correctly, you can at any time have a count estimate for your meetings.

Now let's laugh at that last statement and face reality: many people won't use it correctly, no matter what you do or how easy you make it. That's either because it doesn't hit their personal radar as to being important; or when their status changes, they don't have a device nearby to log in and correct their status; or their status changes very close to the time of the meeting. After all, unless your group drives their primary income or delivers an extraordinary benefit, it has to fit in with the other responsibilities of their lives. A late project at work, a sick child, a fight with a spouse...any number of things can change their ability or motivation to attend your group meeting.

That's why you should continually encourage people to use the RSVP system as it was designed. Because an accurate attendance RSVP doesn't really benefit them, you have to find a way to make it important enough that they do it anyway.

Here are some suggestions to help get them to use the system:

- **Explain the importance to the group overall.** Outline the benefits to both the group and the members personally when they use the system. Recall the previously covered power of the word *because*. Offer them good reasons for using the system. Some of your justification may include:
  - *Because the group wants to provide sufficient seating for everyone.* Nobody likes walking into a room to find that there's no place to sit, especially if they happen to be walking in late. With advance notice on the number attending, you can have the appropriate seating available, even for those that wander in after the meeting begins.
  - *Because the group won't waste printing and can ensure sufficient materials are available.* If your group uses handouts or other materials during the meeting, you often can't get additional copies at the last second. You don't want to waste the time and money on excess materials; their use of the RSVP system can help the group avoid wasted materials and minimize the money waste that results from excess materials.
  - *Because everyone likes having accurate name badges and sign-in sheets.* When you provide pre-printed name tags for people, members always feel a little bit left out when they have to write their own. Emphasize that by RSVPing in a timely manner, *their name tags will be waiting for them.*
  - *Because (if you have food service) the restaurant wants to provide the optimum amount of wait staff.* Nobody wants to get mediocre service in a restaurant. RSVPs mean the restaurant knows how many servers are needed and your meals will come *faster* (one of the other five power words we discussed).

- **Try guilt.** Since the beginning of time, mothers of all nationalities have found guilt an effective motivator. Remind people how much work it is to put together these meetings and that it makes it easier for you personally when they RSVP in advance, as opposed to just showing up.
- **Plead.** Beg them from any other personal perspective you can construct.

Tracking your attendees is important

The goal of the RSVP system is to give you the knowledge on attendance to help you prepare for the meeting and to manage the ongoing functions of the group. But no matter how many people do use the RSVP system correctly, it won't give you perfect information on who actually did attend.

Knowing who actually did and did not attend your meetings can offer great insight into the successes and challenges of your group. It reveals the overall popularity (or lack thereof) of specific presentation topics. It can offer information on advantages or challenges associated with meeting times or specific dates if your groups changes them around. And aggregating that information at a member level can give you perspectives on individual members' interests and preferences regarding the group.

My groups' experience is that about 60-75% of those that RSVP they will attend actually do. The rest are no-shows. Then we have 25-33% of attendees who may show up without an RSVP. I never complain about that: I *want* people showing up to the meetings. But that makes it harder to track who actually did and did not attend. Making an additional effort to track attendees at the meeting itself is important.

Track attendees with a sign-in sheet

Meetup offers an easily printable sign-in sheet option, Print attendee list, within each Meetup meeting under the tools option.

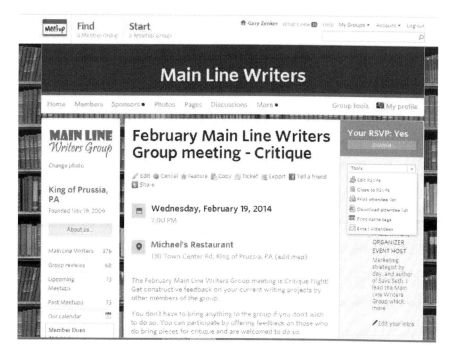

My groups opt not to print the photographs with the name because it creates an unnecessarily long printout which wastes paper.

The resulting list prints the meeting title, the meeting background information as listed in Meetup, the meeting location information, and a list of group members included and sorted in the way you indicate. You can list all members with their RSVP or, as we do, just list the people who RSVP YES or MAYBE. We choose only YES RSVPs to conserve paper and keep the list to a reasonable length. Given up to 40 people showing up out of a 370+ membership, it seems the only practical way of doing it. Those who show up without RSVPing write in their names.

We try to keep the sign-in sheet by the door for people to check off their names as they enter and add their email addresses. Many times, the list ends up being passed around the tables, as well.

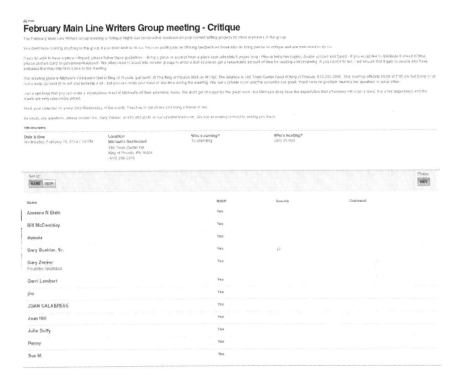

On this list, I often hand-write on the right-hand side whether people are or are not members and their expiration date. We'll discuss the value of this labor-intensive effort under Monetizing The Group.

We ask attendees to both indicate that they attended and give their email. Why should you bother getting emails from members when you can already send email to them through Meetup? Here are several good reasons:

- If the attendees are guest of another member, that guest won't necessarily be a part of your Meetup group, and you will have no way of contacting them directly.
- Meetup doesn't allow you as the sender to include attachments, which may be something you would like to do in some instances.

- Some people block all Meetup incoming mail (either on purpose or by accident) or it ends up in their spam. Your direct email address may not be blocked.

It makes sense to ask for the email addresses at every meeting because people sometimes change email addresses, like when they change Internet service providers. Often, people don't send out notices that they have changed their email address, so you never know about it until….you try to send them something and it fails to arrive. By then, it's too late and you may not have any other way to easily contact the person. So getting an update each time they show up at a meeting is a very good thing. Having an out-of-date list is the same as having no list at all.

There are always going to be a few people who don't or won't sign in. If they are new people, it can be hard to remember after the meeting who they were. So….

Always prepare name tags

I prepare name tags as close to the meeting time as possible (hopefully just a few hours before the meeting is to be held) and strongly encourage people to wear them during the meetings. Name tags perform multiple positive functions for the group members and the group leader.

- **It helps people connect better.** With new people joining our group at every meeting, not everyone knows each other. Wearing name tags, they can greet and address each other by name. They can avoid that terrible moment where one person forgets another person's name (it's an especially bad moment for the group leader). It helps build the relationships between people faster.
- **It helps brand the group and add value.** The tags generated by Meetup allow me to put the group name on the tags. It also

makes it look like the leader pays attention to many details. But this detail is auto-generated for me by the Meetup System.

- **It helps a leader identify those who actually came to the meeting. It also identifies those who RSVPed 'YES' but did not show up**. And because people come who didn't RSVP or did so after the tags are generated, always bring extra blank tags. Remind those who need the blanks that if they sign up earlier next time, their name will be printed on their tags. That can lead to better meeting counts in the future.

Meetup generates the tags as printable, full-sheet PDF files. You have a number of options regarding what information you would like to appear on the tags.

The file generated is compatible with AVERY 5395 tags or compatible stock from other paper companies. Or you can print the file to full-page sticker stock and cut them out yourself. You should test the stock you intend to use with clothing before you do it: not all sticker stocks adhere well to clothing. Many are actually poor in that function.

The files generated can include or omit the red color (shown to the left in grey), as shown:

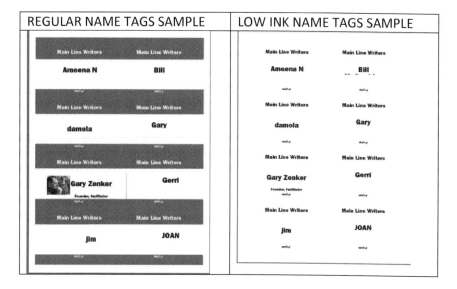

Note that the member name appears on the tag as it appears in the members' profiles. You can't do anything to change that on your end. If they used all caps, it will come out with all caps, if they used only their first name or a nickname...well, you get the idea.

Sticker stock recommendation. I highly recommend the Post-it 2800-N Name Badge adhesive labels with a cautionary warning. I recommend the labels because they have a wonderful sticky surface which adheres better to most clothing (and removes cleanly with no sticky residue) when applied once and not moved. They are also thin and seem to bend better than typical paper labels. As a result, they bend with clothing movement as opposed to resisting it and separating from the clothing.

The cautionary warning is this: the Post-it tags have the excess surface area surrounding the actual tags removed; that is, the area surrounding the tags themselves is the shiny, non-stick surface backing paper with no paper covering. When you print the standard name tag that Meetup generates, the red ink prints onto the non-stick backing paper surrounding the tags, onto which it doesn't really absorb and smears across the name tags. The same is true for the toner when laser printing the Post-it labels. To use these tags, you MUST select the LOW INK option when creating the tags, which eliminates the color bands seen on the example.

Bring extra blank name tags

Don't forget that those folks who don't RSVP and show up anyway also need name tags. So bring extra blank tags. Because the tag printing process creates whole numbers of pages only, it will fill in anything less than a multiple of eight with name tags having only the group name. But if you have 23 RSVPs, that leaves only one blank tag at the end.

One solution is to always bring an extra sheet or two of completely blank tags with the printed tag. But if you want blank tags with your group name on them, go to the Printing Options and deselect *include member names*, *include member photos* and *include member titles/roles*. You will end up with name tags containing only your group name on them. And always pack a sheet or two of completely unprinted tags just in case.

Review the leftover name tags and sign-in list at the end of the meeting

THE RSVP list tells you what your members' attendance intentions were, but not what they really did. Reviewing the leftover name tags and sign-in list tells you about their actual behaviors. Leftover tags should be people who didn't show...

TRACKING INDIVIDUAL ATTENDANCE

So what should you do with all this information about member attendance? Use Meetup to help keep track of it all.

Along the right edge of the event page, Meetup shows who RSVP'd to attend. As facilitator, you can go in and change their attendance status before or after the meeting using the pull-down menu at the top of the right column.

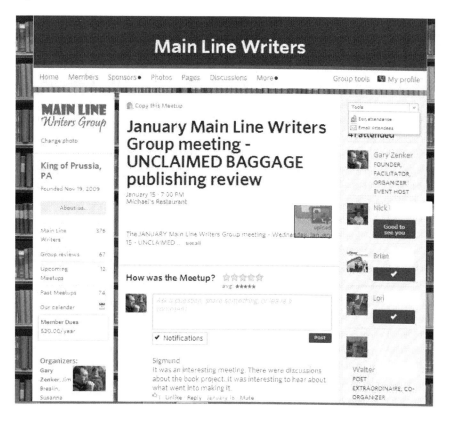

Selecting that option allows you access to the individual members' data, where you can actually change their attendance status.

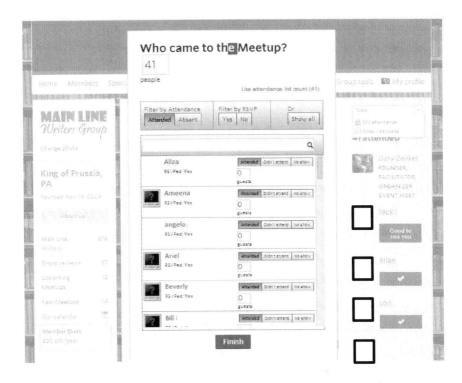

Following a large meeting, it can be hard to remember the details of who was there and who wasn't. This system gives you a fast way to ensure that you have accurate data about the group when you do start analyzing the group attendance.

Why go to all the trouble?

So why go to all this (time-consuming) trouble to track attendance? Primarily because of what it reveals about the individuals within your group and about the programming you are offering.

You may have groups of individuals who are frequent no-shows. By their RSVPs, they look like good members; but in reality, they may not be. Likewise, you may have people who always attend but never RSVP. These are active members who just can't seem to learn to use the RSVP function.

From an individual member standpoint, you can more clearly see what meetings and programming is relevant to individual members. You can use that information to prioritize how much effort you make in regards to specific individuals. A quick note telling them that you missed them and they'll be amazed how much you care specifically about them.

From the wider group standpoint, you can compare the relative attractiveness of your programming. This can guide your efforts in the future to attract a larger group, or focus on the group you prefer to attend.

MANAGING YOUR GROUP PROGRAMMING

SURVEY YOUR AUDIENCE

Remember back to the beginning of this book, where you wrote down your goals for the group. We carefully prioritized the many goals to identify the most important ones and focus efforts to achieve them.

But after you are leading the group for a while, it's easy to have the group head in a direction, subtly or even overtly, that you never intended. Yet, suddenly, things are headed there and you don't know how or when it happened.

Periodic reassessments are an excellent tactic to stay on track.

One of the writers groups' primary goals is to fill the room with involved people. So I survey my members every nine to twelve months on the programming they want at the meetings. Surveying the people who are at the meeting does a couple of things:

- **It rewards them for showing up.** I tell them when I hand out the survey "You are here so your opinion is the most important to this group."
- **It focuses on the most active members.** Since they make the effort to show up, they probably care at least a bit more than those who didn't and continually don't attend. These are the people I want coming back on a regular basis.

It's important to ensure your survey is constructed well and doesn't obfuscate the information you want. The survey we use is simple: a list of program subjects we could offer the group. Members are instructed to pick EVERY topic that they would be interested in attending. I ask them NOT to bother ranking them...it takes too long and requires too much thought. This is supposed to be a fast five minute survey. They mark every topic for which they would attend a presentation. They can also add any others that I did not list.

A typical survey looks like this:

Main Line Writers Group
June 2013 Programming Survey

Name _____

Please place a check mark next to EVERY program you would be interested in attending!

RELATED TO THE WRITING PROCESS
- ☑ Legal & copyright issues related to writing
  - What you can be sued for
  - Work for hire contracts
  - What are your rights
  - Others
- ☑ Online writing communities

- ☑ Software tools for writers
  - MS Word alternatives
  - Submission tracking
- ☐ Workshops and conventions
- ☐

TYPES OF WRITING
- ☑ Blogging
- ☐ Business writing
- ☐ Freelancing

- ☐
- ☐

WRITING DEVELOPMENT
- ☑ Self-editing techniques
- ☑ Character Development
- ☑ Plot Development

- ☐ Humor
- ☐

OTHER
- ☐ Interactive writing session
- ☐ Social-only meeting

- ☐
- ☐

PUBLISHED WRITERS TO TALK ABOUT THEIR PROCESS/SUCCESS
- ☑ Sci Fi
- ☐ Memoir
- ☐ Poetry
- ☑ Journalist
- ☐ Romance
- ☐ Non-fiction
- ☐ Young Adult
- ☐ Children's Lit

- ☐ Thriller
- ☐ Comic Books
- ☑ Historical Fantasy
- ☑ Action/Adventure
- ☐ Horror
- ☐
- ☐
- ☐

Note that we do ask people to put their names on the surveys. There's a good reason for that: if I want to ask some follow-up questions, I can actually go to the person. We've never had a negative response to that request: 100% of the survey takers fill in their names.

The surveys go into a pile and aren't looked at until after the meeting. Once home, I open an Excel spreadsheet and type in the information.

Every positive vote for a topic counts as one. I just total them up from the individual sheets. The patterns become clear quickly and I know what programming should theoretically support the best attendance.

	A	B	C	D	E	F	G	H	I	J	K	L	M	N	O	P	Q	R	S	T	U	V	W
1	**Wilmington Writers Group**																						
2	*Survey first meeting - nov 2013*																						
3																							
4			YES	NO																			
5	Belong to other writers groups?	10	10																				
6	Previous critique?	11	9																				
7																							
8			TOTAL																				
9	**TOPICS**																						
10	RELATED TO WRITING																						
11	Legal		13	1	1	1			1		1		1	1	1	1		1	1		1		
12	Online writing communities		6	1	1	1	1		1		1			1									
13	Software Tools		9	1					1			1	1	1		1	1		1	1		
14	Word Skills		9	1					1			1		1	1	1	1	1	1	1		
15			0																				
16	TYPES OF WRITING		0																				
17	Blogging		9	1		1	1		1	1		1			1		1					1
18	Business Writing		3						1	1				1								
19	Freelance Writing		12	1		1	1	1			1	1	1			1	1	1			1
20			0																				
21	WRITING DEVELOPMENT		0																				
22	Self Editing Techniques		14	1	1	1		1	1	1	1		1	1	1		1	1	1	1		
23	Character Development		11	1		1		1		1	1	1	1	1		1	1	1			1
24	Plot Development		12	1		1		1		1	1	1	1	1		1	1				1
25	Humor		11	1		1	1	1		1		1	1	1	1	1				1
26	Writing Cues		8	1				1			1	1	1		1				1
27			0																				
28	PUBLISHED WRITERS		0																				
29	Action/Adventure		4		1					1		1	1							
30	Children's Literature		4									1	1	1	1				
31	Comic Books		5			1				1	1			1	1			
32	Historical Fiction		9		1	1		1		1		1	1	1	1		1
33	Horror		4							1	1		1	1		
34	Journalism		8		1		1	1	1	1		1	1	1		
35	Memoir		5	1	1			1		1					
36	Poetry		3							1		1		
37	Fantasy		6	1	1					1	1		1	1	
38	Literary Fiction		8			1	1	1		1	1		1		1
39	Romance		1	1										
40	Sci Fi		9		1	1	1			1	1		1	1	1
41	Thriller		3					1			1	1		
42	Young Adult		3	1						1	1		
43	Non-Fiction		8	1		1	1	1				1	1	1
44	Inspirational		3	1						1	1	
45	Self Help		4	1				1	1		1	
46	Business Writing		5			1	1	1		1	1	1	
47	Mystery		6		1		1		1	1	1		1
48			0																				
49	PUBLISHING RELATED		0																				
50	Social Media for Writers		11	1		1	1		1	1	1		1		1	1	1
51	Query Letter Writing		11	1	1			1	1	1	1	1	1	1	1
52	Literary Agent		10	1	1		1	1	1	1	1	1	1	1
53	Self Publishing		9	1		1	1	1	1			1	1	1
54			0																				
55	OTHER PROGRAMS		0																				
56	Critique		13	1	1	1	1	1		1	1	1	1	1	1	1	1
57	Interactive writing sessions		13		1	1		1		1	1	1	1	1	1	1
58	Social Only Meetings		6	1	1			1			1	1		1

By doing this survey process every nine to twelve months, it makes a strong statement to the members that this is THEIR group and what they say has a strong influence on what we do. It keeps the membership involved…it also gives me a comparison to see whether the interests of the group have changed over time. Since we have developed an active core that keeps coming back, they should be less likely as a whole to want the same thing that was offered six months ago. If I try to always offer newbies the most elementary programs, I know I will lose my core group. So even when we repeat topics, we select new presenters and new angles to present the information.

Survey the no-shows, too

I also do a survey for those people who haven't shown up in a while or ever, but I focus on different questions because I am looking for different information from this group. A lot of people will sign up for the group and NEVER show up in person. So I ask them specifically why they don't come to the meetings.

The reason they don't show up varies: typically, those that bother to offer information give statements along the lines that they are no longer living in the area, they are taking a class on that night, or they have other conflicting commitments. I sort through them and look for patterns that may help with the way I run the group or schedule meeting dates and times.

I don't survey no-show members on anything regarding programming. This may initially seem at odds with my desire to get people to attend. But I have found that no-shows sometimes have strong opinions on what they would like, but offering it to them doesn't mean that they are any more likely to show up. They just like to state their opinions, loudly and often. And altering programming to cater to people who have not shown up even once is generally a poor investment in time and effort.

We are always seeking ways to improve the group. Sometimes a great idea surfaces from just one person's suggestion, but I am also wary of "surveys of one." I take those ideas and float them in front of a larger group of members to discover whether they will drive group interest or are very limited in scope. Like anything in life, it makes no sense to chase the group's outer fringe unless that is specifically what you want as a leader and aligns with the goals of your group.

Polls are an option under the More menu option and allow you to survey your entire membership on topics of your choosing. I seldom use them for programming consideration because of the large number of people who belong to the group but never show up to meetings in person.

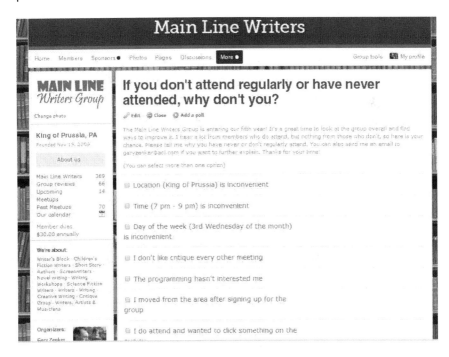

You could use the logic that those people are also least likely to answer a poll...or you might make the argument that discovering what would influence their attendance is valuable information. But, once again, I figure that if they have never even bothered to show up once, changing the programming won't really help: there's some other factor prohibiting their attendance.

Remember that open-ended questions are harder to compare the resulting data, and what you are seeking is a way to group the data so that you can draw logical conclusions and take action on them. Questions with specific answer options can help an organizer understand which concerns are really common issues.

In the few polls attempted, the overall response numbers were extremely low versus the numbers I get from an in-person meeting - 100%. E-mails to the group asking the question of why people fail to attend received more direct responses than the polls. But try it for yourself if you like...maybe your results will be radically different than mine.

Once the poll is set up, you need to send out a group email with a link to the page. Set a definitive end date and don't give people too much time. If they don't have time to take a five minute survey in seven days, what it really means is that they don't have interest in taking a survey. Your odds of getting a completed survey by giving them another week is slim.

MANAGE YOUR PRESENTERS UP FRONT

I can honestly say that we've never had a bad presentation by a speaker...but some have been better or stronger than others. The strongest presentations have always been the result of careful planning and review of the presentation elements.

We vet all presenters up front. I feel personal responsibility that all presentations run smoothly. For that reason, we never invite anyone to speak unless someone in the core group (the frequent attenders) has personally seen them present. There are lots of wannabes in life, and yes, we may have missed a few good people because no one in the group has personally seen them speak (but hey, we have a lot of years left in us). But every presenter we invite in has been vetted by someone I trust. That's a critical component in managing the presentations.

A presentation outline and review is mandatory. As group facilitator, I NEVER ever let someone present without reviewing their outline and talking it over with them. I don't care how good their reputation is, I know the group better because our presenter isn't part of the group. So I ask for an outline up front, before or as I write the description for the session. Nobody wants an exact repeat of the presentation we had six months ago. I offer the speaker insights into the group up front and offer suggestions on "must includes" in what they do. And you know what? Every one of them has been grateful for the direction given. They all want to have a successful session.

Take an active role in the flow of the session. If the presentation strays too far from the outline, or if the crowd looks bored or disengaged and the presenter doesn't adjust, the leader needs to help. Ask questions to bring the presenter back to point or even better, ask a question to someone in the audience to prime them to ask the question. Think of it as the "man behind the curtain" pulling a couple of strings innocuously. Sometimes that's all it takes to move things back on course.

Ultimately, trust the group itself. They are good people who are there for positive reasons: to learn and to share. Unless the group's conversation becomes ego-driven, even the questions focused on individual needs or curiosities often apply to others in the room. When they don't, other members frequently help get the conversations back on track without additional involvement.

COMPENSATING YOUR PRESENTERS

Every group is different. Whether you compensate your presenters in cash or in some other way depends on your group, the presenter, and the value they bring to the meeting.

It should be noted that the presenters at our regular monthly meetings do not receive any money to attend. They know this as they are booked for the presentation. However, because we are holding the event at a restaurant, the group does pays for their meals. And I should mention that in a number of cases, the presenter brings a spouse or a child for a variety of reasons. I pay for their meals also, which pleasantly surprises some of our guests. The speaker is there at the group's invitation: I want him or her and the guest to feel good about how we treated them, not have mixed feelings because they had to pay for a meal for their guest out of their own pockets.

Depending on the distance they travel, the time they travel, or other factors, you may want or need to compensate your presenters for gas, tolls, or even offer some other stipend.

Our presenters agree to come without being paid for a number of reasons. One reason is that they want to help others. They often feel important being asked to speak on their particular specialty or skill. They like having a ready-made, qualified and interested audience. With a range from 26 to 45 members at the meetings, the group can provide them that and it offers a real value.

And they also agree to present for another important reason: many of them offer a service or have written books that they would like to sell directly or indirectly related to the topic on which they are speaking. They are encouraged to bring their books and ad materials. But they are also given this direction: *if people think you are selling, they will immediately tune you out*. The presenter's area of expertise in their area and presentation will make the sale of the product or service. The presentation can be about your process of creating something, on their area of expertise, but it can't be a presentation focused on *selling* it.

That restriction is one of the reasons that someone in the group needs to have seen the person present. By inviting only those people who clearly understand the rules of these kinds of presentations, I don't have to worry about policing their presentations.

OTHER NON-MONITARY COMPENSATION

As a good host, it's your job at the end to do a bit of promotional work for the presenter, to talk about them in a way that they should not do themselves. Do it for them. Tell people about their service or book or whatever they have available to purchase in a respectful and honest way. Third party endorsement is always powerful.

Email and hand-written thank you notes are important. I send out the email the day after the presentation and mail the hand-written note a few days later. These people gave up their time to share their expertise to your group and offer valuable insights. Formal thank-you's are the least you can do.

Offering written recommendations, endorsements and public 'thank-yous' on social media sites including Facebook and LinkedIn are also a great way to show your appreciation. It offers the presenter public credibility and you would be surprised how few people go to the effort.

I want to note that there are some instances in which my group does monetarily compensate speakers/instructors. I created a series of writing workshops for the Main Line Writers Group, separate from the general meetings and requiring an attendance fee. In this case, the presenter is given a portion of the evening's proceeds. Members easily understand and accept that to get an instructor for this content, the instructor needs to be compensated.

Selling *without selling*

Here's one example of how it worked for our group. A recent speaker to the Wilmington Writers Group, Kathryn Craft, is a well-respected editor and now published novelist who presented the ten elements that make up a confident and believable voice for an author. Her introduction included the fact that she just published a book and that she does editing for hire. That's what gives her credibility to make the presentation in the first place: she's a professional who knows her (excuse the obvious pun) craft. But her presentation focused entirely on the topic at hand. Only at the very end did she read the introduction from her newly published novel *as an example of the voice creation.*

Kathryn sold eight copies of her book T*he Art of Falling* to the fourteen attendees of the new Wilmington Writers Group and would have sold more but she sold through all of the copies she brought with her. Those are phenomenal numbers, given that *most of those people attending don't normally read her genre.* She would not have sold any more copies by focusing on the book itself. She created a market for herself as a writer, but also as an editor. That's important because every one of those attending have the potential for needing to hire an editor for their own work, at a much higher profit point for her.

Another significant point is that this wasn't my first experience with Kathryn; she is on a short list of presenters to bring to my groups on a regular basis (which given our meeting frequency means every couple of years). She's easy to understand, speaks on a variety of topics and people walk away from her presentations marveling at the quality of presenters the group offers. I discovered her while she was presenting for a different group. I've now had her to both of the writers groups I run and offered her name to people who have asked me for referrals to editors. That's what happens when leaders find a great resource. They recommend them to other leaders and use them over and over again.

Contrast this with a group I attended where the group leader hosted a start-up company who presented their very attractive specialized videography service. They had a huge line of people signing up and offering their charge cards for $89 charges despite a botched presentation. It took six months to get the company to complete the work they contracted to do and they never really completed the full scope service they offered.

The group leader should be extra careful to ensure that the presenters are credible and can deliver on what they say they will. Whether in this instance it is the fault of the screening process or the presenter, I will always have a doubt in my mind as to the services being recommended or presented by the group. And while you might say that the responsibility lies with the attendees, As Mom always told me, "You are judged by the company you keep." Make sure you do adequate due diligence on your chosen presenters.

END YOUR MEETINGS WITH A SUMMARY

Research reveals that memories are greatly affected by what happens at the end of an experience. There's a great presentation on that topic by Daniel Kahneman that everyone who leads groups or offers services to other people should watch and listen to it: http://www.ted.com/talks/daniel_kahneman_the_riddle_of_experienc e_vs_memory.html

In the presentation, Daniel talks about the research done on the difference between their experience and the memories people retain about that experience, and why they differ. One of the differentiating factors is that which occurs *at the end* of the experience. What happens at the end can change a positive experience to a negative one, despite the negative experience at the end being very brief compared the amount of the time the positive experience lasted.

You can better ensure that people remember the positive take-aways of the meeting by summarizing them at the end of the meeting.

Even better, at the end of each meeting, *have the group memb*ers offer their most important memory points by asking them to tell the group what they found most valuable. Not only will it sound better coming from them, but it also acts as a fast survey without having to take the time to hand around and complete a written page (which can be a valuable option, as well).

PREPARING FOR THE UNEXPECTED

Despite your best planning efforts, things can go in directions you never thought they would. It might be a presenter not showing up despite confirming the day prior; a laptop that worked at home which suddenly refuses to start at your meeting, or even an unexpected guest who is likely to create a disruption.

Welcome to the life of a meeting leader. Anyone who has managed meetings can share a variety of events that happened to them, or a friend, or a friend of a friend. And while you won't be able to prepare a contingency for every possible disaster, there are a few things you can do that will go a long way in helping you deal with a variety of unexpected surprises.

Have an alternate program prepared. Having a program that you can implement at any time is great insurance against unexpected and surprise occurrences. This might be as simple as a discussion topic that you have thought through ahead of time. Or it could be a presentation complete with handouts that you carry to meetings as a back-up.

For the writers groups, we carry an outline for a discussion on copyright law. My work in various industries has exposed me to many of the specifics and, while not a lawyer, I have a good understanding of the implications to writers, artists, and the specifics surrounding publishing. A ready-made summary sheet for handout and a presentation that can be presented from either a laptop or iPad is your insurance policy.

This presentation stays in the bag until I absolutely need it. It's not that the group wouldn't benefit from it, but with only twelve meetings a year, I can plan it and leave it there...and the details of copyright law aren't going to change anytime soon.

Group co-leader and accomplished author Tony Conaway always carries one of his own written pieces, as well as a currently published book with notations as something that can be read to the group and critiqued on the fly. He constantly reminds me that group leaders should always have a backup program planned.

Tony knows quite a bit about leading groups and what could unexpectedly change a meeting. Besides being the co-author of the popular *Kiss, Bow, or Shake Hands* business books (with something like nine editions!), Tony has served in every position of the Brandywine Valley Writers Group with several terms as President. He also runs a comedy club where comedians appear before alcohol-fed guests. He's the guy who can predict the unpredictable.

Your back-up solution might be to merely create a one page outline on a discussion that is relevant to the group. Or you could prepare an entire presentation with handouts and even a multi-media component. But whatever you do for your group, your goal is to be prepared for equipment failure, presenter absence or anything else that would derail the meeting plans and necessitate a change in programming.

Another back-up strategy could involve a spontaneous presentation on from one or more group members who are experts on a particular topic. Even without handouts or a Powerpoint file, members with a passion and expertise can often deliver engaging presentations on the spot. Depending on the group, examples might include recounting attendance at recent conventions or events, a review of recent books or articles of a topic related to the group, or even a follow-up on a recent presentation.

Surprise visitors. In addition to planning for presenters who might not show up, you'll also want to plan for people who do show up unexpected.

It's a great compliment when your members come to you, especially when their own plans change at the last minute. That change may involve a tag-along child. Then reality sets in....how do you maintain decorum and keep your meeting on track?

The answer is **distraction!** Once again, prior preparation is the key. While you may hope that the parent would bring the things he or she needs to keep the child busy, the parent may not have had time to grab anything except the child. Crayons, coloring books and extra paper can be important elements in your Meeting Kit (which we introduce later in this volume) as can an iPhone or an iPad.

Accommodating the parent and the child is a great thing. But if the ongoing presence of a child is disruptive or inhibits the group's functionality, it's up to YOU to have a discussion with the parent.

My group easily tolerates the bi-annual appearance of my son, coinciding with a last-minute cancellation from my sitter. In fact, he is a group celebrity of sorts, the youngest member of the group. But part of that acceptance is no doubt because his daddy is the group leader. I am always ready to take my son out of the meeting room after my introductions are complete if his behavior warrants removal. It's not easy to predict how a five to eight year old will behave on any given evening. Even with a stack of things to occupy him, it can be challenging.

How will you know if the child presents a real problem in your group? It depends on the nature of the group and the nature of the members. Many people won't be forthcoming to you. They won't want to appear to be the child-hating type. It's a good idea to have a private discussion with some of the members to get their take on it. Being asked directly, they are a lot more likely to give you an honest and forthcoming answer.

As with any other meeting element, your responsibility is to the group as a whole. When member behaviors cause major disruptions, you'll need to address them with the individual...in private.

USING YOUR MEETUP.COM RESOURCES

The folks at Meetup continually upgrade and modify its structure and capabilities. They also apply successful strategies and approaches from other applications and social media venues to help organizers create a user-friendly and member-involving construct. Here are some of the functions on which you will want to place focus.

Encourage conversations with messaging

The goal of your group, both in person and online, should be one of engagement. Engagement leads to more people being attracted to your Meetup and more people attending your in-person meet-ups.

The ability to leave messages that others can read is an important part of engagement in the time between the actual in-person meetings. Members can leave thoughts, ask questions and continue interaction with members.

Don't be terribly disappointed if interaction is limited. Creating strong interaction is a challenging and time-consuming effort. People have incredible demands on their time and have so many online areas of interaction that your on-line presence may not be where they spend their time, even if they ARE coming to your meetings.

Your goal should be to encourage it and lead some of it where you can. Ask questions. Ask people directly for responses. Lead by example and definitely respond when you see it.

Be timely in your replies

Timeliness in your responses is important, for obvious reasons. The world operates on a much faster time-frame than it ever has in the past. People expect fast answers and to always be connected. A delay of even a few days makes the statement that they are not important enough for you. They may think you are ignoring them.

And given that public posts can be seen by the entire group, delayed responses don't just send a message to the original sender. Monitor the board every day and send responses as quickly as possible. If people draw the conclusion you don't care about the group members, they may feel the same way about the group.

LIKE it a lot

Meetup gives your members the opportunity to leave messages, respond to others' messages and give quick Likes, similar to Facebook. Encouraging your members to use these functions will expand their involvement with the group and with each other. It's a fast way for people to give each other acknowledgement and a virtual pat on the back.

As a leader, you want to check the messages daily and both respond to their comments and LIKE them. Doing so models behavior for others to follow.

CALLING MORE ATTENTION TO YOUR EVENTS

Clicking into an individual event brings you a number of options related specifically to that event.

The FEATURE option places a banner as shown above, both when you go into the event and when you view all of the events together. If you plan a lot of events in advance, it can be hard to differentiate between them at a glance. It also works to highlight your next upcoming event. This option offers focus for the member.

The TICKET function offers the member an opportunity to print out a ticket-shaped form with all the pertinent information on the meeting: location and map, and event summary as you have posted it. This may be important if you have limited attendance or a very special speaker or presentation. It also looks impressive to have an actual ticket.

Requiring attendees to print tickets can serve as another way to manage your attendance. However, don't be surprised if people don't print them. People seldom bring dry cleaning tickets or other similar items with them: they expect that if they have signed up, they have done all that they have to do and you have all the records needed. It will probably take a while to train people to use them. And if you keep acquiring new members...well...you can see what you may be in for.

Export options. Here, you get the option to export the event to a variety of other applications, including Outlook, iCal, Google and Yahoo. You also have the opportunity to export social media messages via Twitter and Facebook.

USE THE LINKS TO OTHER SOCIAL MEDIA

The elements within Meetup help promote and engage the individuals who are already a part of your group. The posts are also visible in a limited fashion to non-members who are a part of the Meetup world. But there's a huge world of people out there, people you know who are NOT part of your Meetup group. You need to get your announcements out to these other potential participants, as well.

Expand the reach for your group announcements and communications beyond your Meetup group by using the social media links from inside your Meetup account management.

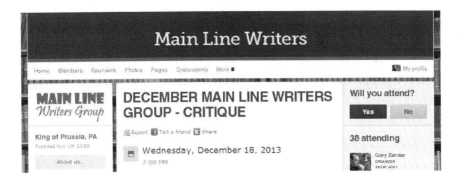

The Facebook icon accesses whichever Facebook account you link to your management profile (this is an important detail if you have more than one). Clicking on it allows you to send notices of events plus header messages to individuals who have friended you or groups to which you belong.

Your group logo is automatically loaded as shown.

The link to your event is placed with the message. Facebook offers a generous 420 character maximum message size where you can add information to the event description.

Note that you are given the option to enter either a friend's name, a group or email addresses.

The Twitter icon performs the same basic functionality for that application. Keep in mind that Twitter has a 140 character limit, far less than the Facebook character limit.

Export allows you to append your Outlook, iCal, Google and Yahoo calendars in a similar way, prefilling the time and date fields. In Google, you can add email addresses for invitees. It's a great time saver in promoting your event to those outside Meetup.

OTHER EVENT MANAGEMENT TOOLS

The right-hand column also holds a pull-down menu labeled TOOLS, which offers a number of important functions for managing the event attendance.

Keep in mind that you can adjust attendance after the event, as well, by notating who said they would attend but didn't and visa-versa. But for some events, tracking who is coming beforehand is vitally important to food counts, seating and other factors.

Edit RSVPs allows you to go into the RSVPs you have and make adjustments to those members for the event only. You may change members' RSVP status, add guests they are bringing. You can even go into individual member data from there and see more general data on the member (number of Meetups attended according to the system, comments, dues paid, etc). We covered this topic in more detail earlier in the book.

Close RSVPs allows you to close down the RSVP function for the event, indicating to people that you are no longer accepting RSVPs. Once closed, the pull-down menu option changes to "Re-Open Event." This is useful when you want to set a definite upper limit to the number of people who can attend. It also has the effect of creating a reason for people to RSVP earlier, to avoid being closed out of an event.

Attendance lists has two options to help you track attendance at the event. **Print attendee list** gives you an event header and a list of attendees (with picture, number of guests and comments if they have placed them online) for use as a management tool or a sign-in list. The **Hide Photos** option minimizes the length of the resulting output, but if you want it all on a single sheet of paper, leaders will want to use the **Download attendee list** option instead. That exports the list to an Excel format, which you can open in Excel, create two or three columns and get the whole thing on a single page.

Print name tags offers the ability to...yes, print name tags in an Avery-standard format (8395, 5395 and 45395. Details on this were covered earlier in the book.

Email Attendees, the file option under the menu, takes you to the email function and prefills the specific event but nothing else. You need to create the rest of the email content yourself.

POST PHOTOS OF YOUR EVENTS

This is another big 'duh', but pictures can tell someone new about your group much faster than words ever can. And let's face it, photos are fun. Even though most people have phones in their cameras and can take pictures themselves, they still enjoy looking for themselves and friends in photos others have taken.

Meetup realizes how important photos are to social media and gives then a permanent home in the **Options** menu, front and center. Photos can be organized into groups, creating better organization and an easier browsing experience.

They've also (wisely) incorporated the same type of tagging function present in Facebook and a number of other social media applications. Tagging is important for numerous reasons.

- It helps people unfamiliar with the group identify people they may already know.
- It gives people another reason to look closer at the photos.
- It encourages participation by giving them the ability to do the tagging themselves

Even with all of that participation encouragement, don't be surprised if as the leader, YOU end up doing most of the tagging. Like any functions, you have to repeatedly request people to do it. The average member does not necessarily have the motivation to go through fifteen minutes of tagging, even though they would be perfectly willing to spend that time looking over the pics.

The tricky part here is that the tagging is based on the name that people used on their Meetup profile. If they only used a first name, that first name is all that will appear in the list of available names *and link back to their profile*. You can still opt to tag people with their full name or with a name not associated with the group, but it won't link back to the person's profile.

All of that said, the tagging function is a great way to encourage the involvement of other members. It gives them something to do that is associated with the group and takes the responsibility out of your hands. It's also easy and doesn't require much technical expertise.

In the illustration above, this photo is from a book launch party and we tagged the mask prop as Victor Von Doom (enemy of the comic book characters The Fantastic Four). There is no Meetup member by the name of Doctor Doom but we were able to tag it anyway for fun (and as an example of tagging). You can tag people in photos that are not part of your group (presenters, guests etc) in the same way. Note that the names of all individuals tagged appear under the *In this photo* line below the photo. The names also appear when the cursor hovers over the person in the photo.

In addition to tagging, photos can be notated with descriptive text.

The photo, like the events, can be shared via Facebook and Twitter buttons just below each photo.

Consider photography to be an important engagement tool for both existing members and for attracting new members to the group.

POSTING VIDEO OF YOUR EVENTS

If a picture is worth 1,000 word, then video must be worth 100 times that...but only if it's interesting. Otherwise just it's an anchor that quickly weighs everything down. Think about watching someone else's home videos...unless they have strong entertainment value or you have some connection to the people in the video, watching them is a waste of your time.

Statistics show that video *can* hold people's interest four to six times as long as anything else on the web. It can give real life to things that are otherwise flat and uninteresting.

Anyone with an iPad or a smart phone can record a video, so documenting the more interesting parts of your Meetup event can be a good tactic. But using the videos straight as-is probably isn't. You'll want to edit them and change angles and scenes, add text for call-out purposes and...generally make them more interesting. Most people have the tools that they need at hand or almost immediately available for a small price. Having the skills or insights to use them is another matter.

Preparing your video. Most people who own a PC also have *Windows Live Movie Maker* available to them as part of the operating system. It allows you all sorts of customizing options, including simple video editing, and the ability to mix video and still photo clips, do zooms and pans, add text etc. You have to learn it well enough to apply the animations for the elements but it is a very self-explanatory application. If you have above average computer skills, exploring it for an hour or two will teach you enough that you can learn enough of the mechanics to plow out something for the group.

Or go to *Animoto.com* online and use their online video builder. There, you upload the photos, select a video style, select a music track and let it rip. Animoto applies the element animation itself and does all of the heavy lifting for you. You can build a video quickly and without a lot of decision making. For many leaders, the time and effort savings is a true blessing.

Their free personal plan gives you a couple of video styles, web quality video and a music library. The most significant limitation is that it will make videos of 30 seconds in length or shorter. You can buy an upgrade to $15/month or $99 a year and create HD quality with videos up to ten minutes. That serves double duty for most organizers, allowing them to also create presentations for the group and is a very reasonable deal. There are other companies that offer similar services…I just haven't used them first-hand to recommend them. You can find them with a simple Google search.

Offering a single video file with a slide show of photos makes the presentation of the photos even more special and requires the viewer to make fewer clicks to see the event. Group member always have a good reaction to these when I create these as a follow-up for the events that have been held.

Mac users are already set with advanced video capabilities and iMovie software built into their systems and should explore those before investing in outside services.

ADD CUSTOM DESIGNED PAGES

This is probably one of the most under-utilized functions in Meetup, perhaps because people don't fully realize it exists! Although the interface isn't as expansive as other web tools, it does offer great flexibility to create something that isn't already a standard Meetup page.

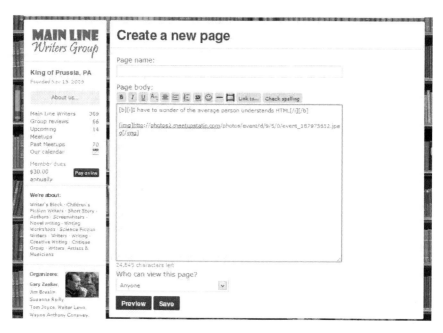

The limited formatting options create the HTML code needed to produce the page. Note that you can't preview the page until you commit to naming it. For those who understand HTML, you can certainly add other HTML 5 code and the page will use it correctly in most cases.

The default options don't allow for type size changes, but you can get a reasonable result with the basics by thinking ahead, as I did here:

One way to circumvent the inherent limitations in type size, etc. is to *create a single full-page graphic.* You won't have any active web links or interactive content, but you will be able to better control the appearance of what is on the page in terms of element placement, type size, etc.

You can also make the entire graphic a link that, when clicked, sends you to another web page. In our case, clicking anywhere on the book graphic sends you to the Amazon page for the book. We could have done the same with the text, but we did that again, separately, at the very end of the text block.

Make sure that when you apply the link or other attributes, you highlight the relevant text or code for the graphic.

POST FILES FOR THE GROUP

Residing beneath the **MORE** menu is a files repository. This is a perfect place to post files for the general welfare of the group or related to presentations made. Files are limited to 10 megabytes in size and allow for a written description. You can set download restrictions to Anyone, Members of the group, or just the Leadership team.

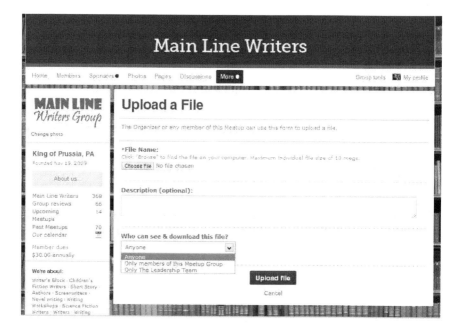

Files are available immediately following their being uploaded. The ability to upload can also be restricted to Leadership only or open to all Members of the group.

Meeting minutes, speaker notes and handouts, additional reading and reference materials are excellent items to make available to your membership through the files area.

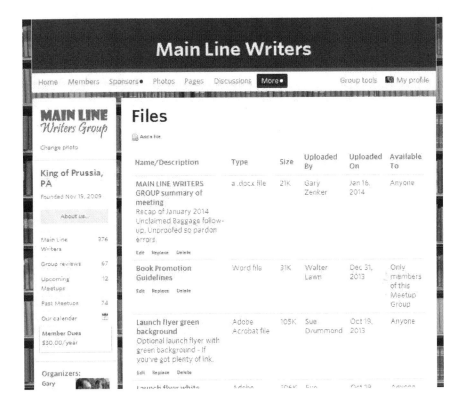

As a leader, you want to manage the upload area carefully. While there's certainly no harm in having a lot of files available, and files are listed in backward chronological order (latest first), you may want to do a periodic clean-up.

One of the challenges is that people don't automatically check out the files section. When you want people to visit it or download files, you need to send them a link through the emails you are sending. Thus, you are best advised to upload the file *before* constructing the email you are sending, and then embed the location link in the body of your email.

USING SUPPLEMENTAL RESOURCES

Meetup is great for what it does... interactive tools for managing a group that meets together. It offers a community where people can opt-in for more info and it manages the ongoing scheduling and communications with your members. It even manages the monetization of the group with relative ease!

But even with all its benefits, Meetup doesn't do it all. The previous example of the limitations that exist on the custom page is one example: you just don't have the full flexibility to create whatever you want, the way you want it to look.

In order to keep things simple for the average person, they've eliminated some capabilities and options. It makes sense, but you may want more. More pizzazz. More flash (well, not the programming language Flash...it doesn't work on iPads and iPhones). More style.

And then remember this, as well: not everyone is part of the Meetup Universe. I'll grant you that Meetup is a large and wonderful community, which is why it is so powerful. It helps guide those who are already part of the community to your group based on their self-stated interests. And it does amazing things as a tool to manage the many time involved tasks of managing a group. It even SEOs well and scores very high as a site on Google. But there's a larger world out there and you should be a part of it.

THE CASE FOR A GROUP WEB SITE

A well-organized and well-structured web site outside of the Meetup structure and site can offer great benefit to your group. It puts a lot of information in an easier to find format, in a format you choose or design.

Building your web site doesn't have to be extremely time consuming or resource intensive. But to create a good and effective site, you need to invest at least a bit of both time and resources. To build your web site, use the following implementation steps. While they are very simplified, following these steps will help you construct a site that offers strong value for your group.

Research other web sites

Find web sites for other sites serving groups like yours. Bookmark them so you can go back to them later. Document what you do and don't like about them.

SITE ADDRESS	WHAT I LIKE	WHAT I DON'T LIKE	NAVIGATION TABS (LIST ALL)

Create a structure for your site

Use your research to create a structure outline for your "perfect" site. Don't worry about graphics or the actual text YET. Your goal is first to create the structure for what your site pages will contain from an overview standpoint; an effective organization of the information you want to present. If you take your time and do this, I promise you will use a tenth of the time to create your site and have a lot less frustration than if you just "wing it".

Many people use the word *wireframe* to refer to a variety of different things. We'll use it here to indicate a website structure and an overview of content included. A typical handwritten wireframe might look like this:

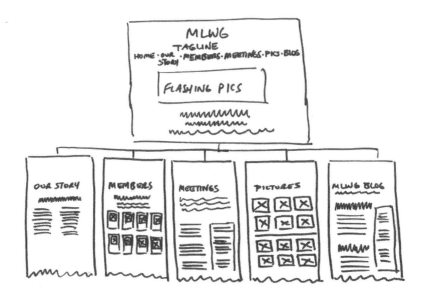

Your "wireframe" should be fairly simple and may get changed after you start the next step (creating an outline for your content). Don't worry if it does. Just go back, make some modifications and continue your work.

Create an outline of your page content

Outline the major categories of what you want to present. But don't write your actual content yet. Your teachers from grade school and high school offered the most important writing lesson in life: always create an outline first.

An outline requires you to think through what you are going to say and what the key points will be. Without an outline, it's easy to start writing and cover lots of things...none of which you needed to communicate. No outline also means that your text may ramble or miss the points it needs to make. Lack of an outline generally means you will spend much more time than was required to finish your project.

Well written content is organized, targets a specific audience (as opposed to what the writer wanted to say) and communicates clearly. That **sounds** easy because we have all been writing since the first grade or earlier, and few people believe that they write or communicate poorly. Despite that belief, success requires careful work.

Here's one example of an effective outline and the level of detail that is appropriate for a web page:

Main Line Writers Group: OUR STORY

- Welcome statement
  - What we do
  - When we meet
- Monthly programs
  - Bi-monthly programming
  - Bi-monthly critique
- Bonus Critique program
- Attend as you like
- See our schedule
  - RSVP
  - Link to Meetup
- Contact for questions

Write your content

Now, with outline in hand, start writing your copy. Reading from a computer screen is a little different than reading from paper. For example, many screens are oriented horizontal as opposed to vertical, so you see less at one time than you do on a piece of paper which is oriented vertically.

Given the differences in reading, here are a few quick hints that are important when writing for the web.

- Keep your sentences relatively short.

- Keep your paragraphs to five lines or less where possible. Longer paragraphs confuse the eye when it tries to move from the end of one line to the beginning of the next.
- Use sub-heads at least every two or three paragraphs. It's a great tool for summarizing a central idea or theme. It also helps in long passages to further break the text into readable "chunks".

Edit, edit, edit

The worst communicators are those who fall in love with their own words. They tend to write for themselves and forget that the main goal of the words is *communication to another party*. When the audience doesn't understand the concepts being communicated, that writer often blames the reader. And even when the blame is reasonably placed, the end goal of clear communication is lost. If you want to communicate something to readers, you have to *respect their intelligence and their limitations*.

After writing a draft, put the text away for a short while and come back to it with a fresh perspective. After you think you have it in a fairly finished form, show it to others and ask them very specific questions:

- Was it clear or confusing?
- Did it hold your interest?
- What did you get out of it?
- What other questions did you have after you read it?

When they provide feedback, SHUT UP. LISTEN to what they say. Your only interruptions should be to ask for clarification on specific comments and points they are making. Don't become defensive about your wording. Later, you can decide whether or not you use the suggestions that they made. These people are giving you two very valuable things: their time and their opinions. Show them your appreciation by offering them the respect of LISTENING to them. There's nothing more insulting than asking someone for their opinion and then discrediting it as they give it.

Walter Lawn, a very intelligent writer, friend, and Main Line Writers Group member, gave me the best writing advice I have ever heard. Paraphrased: "If multiple people tell me there is a problem in an area of my writing, I may not make the change they suggest but I realize I probably have to do something with that part of my writing." I hope you will embrace his very wise advice.

Find graphics and text to enhance your written content

All of what is discussed here applies not only to creating a web site, but also to anything you produce for your group.

The web offers a lot of existing content, both written and visual. Given that, it's tempting to borrow that content, with or without acknowledgement of the source.

But keep in mind that you don't have the legal rights to just grab and use whatever you find on the web. You can't just go into Google or Flickr, search for posted images or videos, then grab and use whatever you find there. Anything created by someone else has copyrights attached to it, whether they choose to exercise them or not. The ability to use these works depends on a variety of factors. Even if there is no copyright notice indicated on content from the internet, odds are that it is covered in some way by copyright.

You may have found the content in some way where the copyrights don't show up on the page you are browsing. Or the content may be included on that other site illegally. Using it subjects you to the penalties of copyright violation regardless.

Copyright concerns

A full discussion of copyright is beyond the scope of this book. But here are a few facts of which you should be aware. This should not be considered legal advice and you should reference the original copyright law documents for a full understanding of the law or seek legal advice:

- The U.S. Copyright Law has changed several times and the facts people quote you may not be in line with the latest legal definitions. You can check them for yourself at: http://www.copyright.gov/
- Anything originally published before 1922 in the U.S. is generally considered in the public domain because all copyrights and copyright extensions as permitted by law have expired. Items published (and unpublished) after that but before 1964 may also be in the public domain, depending on a number of circumstances, including whether or not the original copyright was renewed and when.
- As a general rule, for works created after January 1, 1978, copyright lasts for the life of the author plus 70 years. For a work made for hire, copyright lasts 95 years from the year of first publication or 120 years from the date of creation, whichever expires first.
- Copyright is effective the moment a work is created and fixed in a tangible form. Under current law, publication is not necessary for copyright protection.
- Copyright registration is voluntary but if you wish to bring a lawsuit for infringement of a U. S. work, you must register the work. Registered work may be eligible for statutory damages and attorney's fees in successful litigation.
- Original authorship appearing on a website may be protected by copyright, including writings, artwork, photographs and other forms of authorship protected by copyright.
- Taking something from a website where there is no copyright notice does not mean it is in the public domain or copyright free. Even if the site itself and its authors don't hold the copyright to the material, it may be there illegally. Taking it from them does not protect you from being in violation of copyright law.
- Even if the original publisher is no longer an active business concern, the rights may have been acquired by another entity. The author may have only sold first serial rights, meaning that

the ownership for the actual text or images reside with the original owner.

The best way to ensure you are legally compliant and not subject to lawsuits is to either license legitimate content or find content that has fallen into the public domain by obtaining it from a legitimate source.

The same basic descriptions hold true for both written and graphic content; the examples here reference graphics and images.

Licensing images and content

Given that the web is a visual medium, you are certainly going to want to include graphics on your web site. Graphics, photography and videos entertain, improve engagement and enhance understanding of your page content.

Depending on the source and what you are seeking, content licensing can be just a few dollars for hundreds of images to hundreds of dollars for a single image. Finding the right image for your use is often time consuming and requires multiple sources.

Software packages sold in stores offer hundreds of thousands of images for one set price. But it's important to check the licensing agreement included. Some packages are only for non-commercial use. Others involve restrictions depending on the usage. From a consumer standpoint, it is up to *you* to understand the type of license being provided and to stay compliant.

There are also a number of online sites providing access to collections of images where you either pay for (virtually) unlimited use over a period of time or license images on an individual basis. The best one for you is the one that best fits your needs.

A Google search on the words *stock photography* or *clip art* will deliver thousands of photographic resources. Here are a few in particular which you may wish to consider:

Dreamstime.com	*Stock photos & images*
Everystockphoto.com	*Stock photos & images*
Fotolia.com	*Stock photos & images*
iStockPhoto.com	*Stock photos & images*
Photos.com	*Stock photos & images*

These services have typically done an excellent job in categorizing and offering keyword searches for their images. You may have the challenge of looking through thousands of images, but your first keyword search is likely to identify those images most likely to match your needs.

Stick to legitimate providers. As the user, you are depending on the software seller to have correctly licensed the images if they themselves are not the original creators. It's easy for anyone to put together collections of outside images and sell them as their own, especially companies out of the country where legal suits might be expensive and difficult to initiate. But if YOU use those images and are in the same country as the copyright owner, you may be an easier lawsuit target. License material from reputable, known companies or web sites like those I have listed to avoid problems.

Public Domain sources for content. Public Domain content involves images and videos where any copyrights have actually *expired* and the pieces have fallen into permanent copyright-free status.

The challenge is finding true copyright-free or public domain images and content. Some web sites allow only non-commercial use of the images or content; others allow any type of use. Some sites offer a combination of copyright-free images and restricted use images. Read the fine print and understand what you actually are seeing.

Appendix A lists a variety of sources for public domain you may want to explore. Keep in mind that public domain sources may be less aggressively indexed than commercial resources and it may take you a lot longer to find the images that are appropriate for your needs. Sometimes, free is a lot more costly than it first appears.

Create your web site

Creating your site involves selecting or creating a visual theme, merging your text and graphics together in a way that tells a story that will interest, engage your readers and make them take the next step (whatever that is).

You can opt to hire a professional to do the work for you or you may want to take a stab at it yourself. If you do want to construct it on your own (either for creative or cost factors), there are many services that make it easy to do it yourself by offering attractive templates (themes).

Going into all the pros and cons for a variety of services is beyond the scope of this book, so I'll just mention a few:

- **WORDPRESS.COM** is popular because it offers a variety of templates and customization options, and it integrates the advantages of a blog environment. The ability to interact through blogs and public comments can be very attractive, especially for a Meetup group, but it also necessitates active management of the resulting site, which is a resource commitment. Of course, you can also create a Wordpress site with limitations on who can comment, limiting your ongoing management requirements.

  Basic Wordpress functionality is free. The publishers and third parties offer a number of options to extend site functionality and a great number of people specialize in programming for the application. These extensions vary in cost and sometimes require an experienced programmer to implement.

- **WIX.COM** is my personal favorite online web site creation environment. Like any application, there's a bit of a learning curve but the program is straight-forward and reasonably easy to use. The numerous templates are very attractive, varied, and organized by business and use categories. Like Wordpress, it offers a lot of functional extensions and allows you to create nearly any kind of site you would like to offer, including ecommerce sites.

Wix integrates nearly every function you can think of into it but requires that you host the site with them. The cost isn't unreasonable and falls in line with most other online offerings.

PRINTED COLLATERAL

In addition to the promotional efforts you make on the web, you'll probably need to supplement them with other efforts involving traditional printing of various types.

Your first instinct may be to print everything off your own home printer, and sometimes that works fine. Normal 8 ½ x 11 fliers can be done the night before you need them from the convenience of your home. But here's a fact you should know: while it may be more convenient, it may not be cheaper to do them that way.

When you go through the trouble of calculating the cost of buying paper, buying the ink and factoring the life of your home printer, it can actually be more expensive than having the printing done for you. Sometimes it's just a little more expensive... or depending on your volume of printing, it may be a lot more expensive.

I love to support local print companies. They are smart people who are relationship focused. I also find that some online digital printer services are good sources, especially when budgets are tight and you need smaller quantities.

The choices you make will depend on the factors most important to YOU.

Here are a few ways to save money on your printing at home or at a print shop:

Fliers. I almost always print these from my own equipment. That's because I typically print less than 30. That's generally below the rate for reasonable discounts on full color digital printing. Also I print on standard white paper because the fliers are disposable and fancy glossy paper and heavier ink coverage don't really make a difference in the message I am sending or how I am distributing these.

Here are some ways you can save money on your printing, whether you print at home or from a print shop/office supply place:

- **Print black ink/toner on colored paper.** Color attracts the eye, but depending on your flier, using colored paper may cost close to the same as a regular ream of paper, but using only black ink may save you a small fortune in your overall printing.
- **Use less expensive paper.** Consider where the fliers are going. High quality thick paper may be irrelevant to their functionality.
- **Explain to the group how the fliers should be used.** After just a few meetings, I found that people were taking the fliers for themselves but not distributing them anywhere. 100% of my members already get their notice from Meetup and don't need a paper reminder. I emphasize that and tell them only to take fliers if they plan to hand them somewhere. Few do and they stopped taking them. I saved time and money on home printing.

Banners and posters. Most people don't have a choice on where to print these: they don't own oversized printers to do these at home. Your only option is to go to a place that does this kind of printing.

I recommend that you stay with standard sizes. You can, of course, create posters in any size that you want. But you also need to think about how you will display what you create. You may think you can hang the posters, but much of the time your locale won't make that easy. You'll need to mount it to foam core or other sturdy backing, or place it in a frame. You can often buy standard size frames at a reasonable price: custom framing is generally priced at a premium. Stick to 16" x 20", 22" x 28" or 24" x 36", or with specialized 18"x 30" or 30" x 60" if you are also using specific poster stands.

A folding easel is a great investment. They are generally light which makes them easy to transport. But when used with a foam core mounted poster, they blow over easily in outdoor situations. A heavier frame actually makes them more stable and helps prevent them from tipping by accident.

When ordering your poster, you will generally be offered paper, indoor and outdoor material options.

Paper is great if you are intending to use it as a temporary poster or place it into a frame. The indoor material is often somewhere between paper and a thin plastic. It rolls and unrolls easily and works great with stands.

The outdoor material is marketed to be more durable but I want to offer a warning: I found that the thicker material, while more durable itself, shows a tendency for the ink to easily scrape off, much more easily than the other materials. If you opt for it, you will probably want to treat the poster with something to protect the ink surface a little better, and ensure that the treatment itself is moisture resistant.

For all posters, invest in a storage tube to void damage during transportation to and from use. The $4 you spend will save you lots of money on poster reprinting.

Postcards, trading cards, book marks and other specialty printing
Depending on the event and the project, you may have other kinds of printing that will help promote your group or event. I do a bit of this type of printing to promote the group or related projects. Our group may attend a book fair (an obvious place to find writers interested in self-development). In these cases, I create generic pieces that I can print in quantity and use them over time. So I look for quality/quantity price

maximization. I have to be willing to distribute tons of these materials and they need to make my group look like it is worth joining.

Printing resources. My number one go-to resource for posters is my local *Staples* retail store. For me, they are convenient, they know me and they guarantee their work. The times that the proof print out I provided didn't match their finished printing, they reprinted it for free. You would expect that, but that's a hard service level to match by mail order and avoids double-paying on postage charges in cases where you need to return something to be redone.

And to be honest, I seldom pay their normal retail price. I plan out my printing and wait for a sale, either in store or online. You can save 60%-70% of the costs by doing it this way: they have sales pretty frequently. I also bring them fliers from other office supply stores and they sometimes match those, as well. They are a great source for posters and banners, and sometimes postcards as well. Note that they do have specials that are exclusively offered online or exclusively in the store. Sign up for their weekly mailings.

Online digital printing prices vary a great deal: some are better buys than your local printers. A few of the services have worked better for me than others. I really like *Ztoone.com.* I like their paper weight, print quality and the varnish they use on the full color pieces. I have ordered **trading cards** from them and they always turn out great. As a bonus, even though 1000 is their minimum quantity, their pricing at 1000 is the same as other printers' 250 or 500.

Moo.com produces gorgeous work but it's pricier. They use a thicker stock and run a velvet-like varnish on the surface of their business cards. These make a strong impression on everyone who sees them...but you have to be willing to spend more: like $139 for just 200 business cards. But wow, what an impression they make.

Strategies to get a better printing price

Here's a trick I learned that sometimes gets me a lower price: stop just short of ordering. A number of these online companies have tracking systems in place to make you offers at lower prices if you didn't complete your order. They figure that if they can't get your business at full price, you might complete the order with a discount offer.

Go through the file upload or online file creation. Give them all of your contact information. Then stop just short of ordering. Wait a few days. I've had offers at half the original quote to complete the order.

Also, if you have already used their intro offer, try creating an entirely new account with the printer with a different shipping address. Often, you will get another intro offer (if they an offer at the time).

Search online for coupon codes. Enter the name of the company and the words Coupon Code into the search engine and go explore the results. Sometimes you can find significant discounts this way. Just be wary of the web sites you go to and have virus protection on your computer: some also have malware or other dangerous files.

Finally, ask the vendor for a lower price. It's a competitive market. Sometimes a simple email stating that you can get the same product cheaper someplace else will result in a lower offer. It's worth trying.

SOUND ENHANCEMENT

If you are lucky, you will find the perfect presentation room with wonderful acoustics and every speaker will project well enough so that even the people in the back corner of the room can hear every word.

Don't depend on being so lucky. Odds are good that unless your group is just six to eight people, you will encounter at least a few challenges regarding sound in the meeting rooms you find available for use.

Many times, the room itself isn't ideal acoustically and you will need to find ways to compensate for that fact. Creative placement of your meeting members is one solution, but even if you have your own private room, there can be a lot of distracting background sounds which leak in from missing ceiling tiles, walls that don't extend to meet the ceiling, or even from open doorways.

If you are meeting in a back or private room, a microphone, amplifier and speakers may be your answer. For your solution, you really want to consider portability, power (wattage) and convenience. Sacrificing any of these can easily have you spending money on a system that doesn't really solve your problem. And your solution will depend on the size of your group and the room that you have. But remember that flexibility should be key: the room you have this month may NOT be the one you have next month.

Sound system recommendations

The Samson XP150 (retailing $299 - $349) is a portable, self-contained PA system that offers the best value I found. The unit has two 75 watt speakers which fit together to carry as a single unit weighing just 24 pounds. All accompanying wires fit inside the unit when carrying.

The unit features a removable power mixer. It is lightweight and features 3 XLR and quarter inch microphone inputs, selectable reverb and channel volume. Channel 4 offers two quarter inch stereo inputs and a 3.5 mm input. There is also a master output and a master EQ. in English, that means it offers more inputs than you will probably need and can even take sound input from your iPod or iPhone. You can adjust sound for each input and then have a separate control for the overall output.

It's more powerful brother (or sister), the Samson XP308i, is a 150 watt per speaker system retailing about $500. It offers 4 microphone inputs. It also offers a fifth stereo input which allows ¼ inch microphone AND

RCA jacks and a number of additional inputs including an iPod doc. It also offers an output RCA jack for recording and two monitor outputs, plus a six LED output indicator.

Both systems are built for, but do not include, speaker stands. Raising the speakers off the ground will improve the quality of the sound and the distance it will carry. But they won't fit inside the speakers themselves. Oh well.

Important sound system considerations

The key to using these or any other PA system units is speaker placement. While your immediate reaction may be to place the speakers up front to either side of the presenter, better placement is often to the side or at the back of the group. The people right up front can probably hear your presenter without enhancement...by placing the speakers on the sides or back of the group, you'll increase everyone's ability to hear. But ultimately, placement will depend on the room itself and from where the background noise originates.

It appears that wire lengths of up to 50 feet are not likely to exhibit much sound loss, especially with voice. And that will handle most small to medium sized indoor groups easily. The Samson systems come with 25 foot speaker wire lengths included. You can buy the longer legth wires for $10-24 each.

But the 25 foot length may easily be enough for most moderate sized groups. Because the breakout box controlling the speakers can be placed virtually anyplace that has power access, you can add flexibility by using wireless microphones. Using a wireless microphone in the presenter's control and the receiver plugged into the mixer input, it really can go nearly anywhere...including behind the crowd.

Seriously consider lapel microphones (wireless or wired) for your primary presenter. Hand-held microphones suffer from movement as your presenter moves around. A couple of inches change in distance from the mouth can make a big difference in the loudness...and create an inconsistency in the audio throughout the presentation.

Many microphones don't need to be attached to the lapel, making their use very flexible.

For a high quality wireless microphone, consider the Sony ECM-AW3. It gets high reviews almost everywhere and I can tell you from personal experience that the range and quality of this microphone and receiver set is excellent. They use standard AAA batteries and a standard 3.5 mm or 1/8" jack. List price is $229.99 but the street price is about $139.99.

Audio Technica makes a VHF and Samson makes UHF wireless microphone systems as well, ranging from $99 to $499 each, in both hand-held and label configurations. I found that having one handheld and one lapel model is offers maximum flexibility. Keep in mind that the electronics gods like to look down and laugh on humans. Always bring backup microphones, the wired kind.

YOUR MEETING TOOLKIT

Having managed endless Annual Stockholder meetings, professional events and a national trade show & convention attendance for a number of companies, I can tell you that *there is one common thread* among them all: at some point, you will need something you didn't expect to need. Worse yet, in many instances, you have to make due with whatever you already have: you won't have the time, manpower or availability to get what you are missing.

Sometimes it's just a minor inconvenience. But other times, it threatens to destroy your entire event or make it look like you have no ability to plan ahead. In either case, a Meeting Toolkit is the solution!

You'll never be able to plan for every contingency: but the good news is that many common problems are easy to plan for, especially if you give yourself a little extra thought time and borrow the experiences of people who have already been through it hundreds of times themselves.

Start with a large plastic, handled container and label it with your contact information. Things sometimes get left behind and...once you get it together, you don't want to lose it for any reason. You may also want to invest in a small folding dolly or cart. Sure, you can be macho (if you are a guy) and haul the whole thing over your shoulder...until you start exhibiting back problems. Do your body a favor and get the folding dolly/cart.

Remember that you may not need the entire list of things presented here...YOU need to determine what things might be needed and what things would never be needed. But also remember that it may not be you that has the emergency...it may be the presenter. Having something that the presenter forgot is also a great benefit of planning ahead.

In addition to the toolkit items, listed here are also things we've mentioned in other parts of the book. It's nicer and more convenient to have it all in one place and one checklist (at least I think so).

DATE CHECKED _____   CHECKED BY _____

MEETING TOOLKIT		
Kit Management		
	Marketing Toolkit Checklist	
Electrical-related		
	Extension Cord/Power Strips	2 Plug polarity adapters
Membership-related		
	2 Sharpie Pens	3" x 5" cards
	3 Regular Ink Pens	2 Pads of lined Paper
	Blank Name Tags	Blank Card Stock
Signage-related		
	8 ½ x 11 Group Name/Logo doors signs	8" x 10" Erasable Marker Board
	Adhesive Tape (Masking and Cellulose)	Erasable Markers
	Bungee Cords	Small magnets
	Zip Ties	Folding Easel
Presentation Equipment-Related		
	Adapter to connect iPad to TV/Monitor	PA System
	Audio 1/8 " male-to-male cable	Conventional Microphones
	Extra batteries (AAA and AA)	Wireless Microphones
	Laser Pointer	¼" to 1/8" audio adapter (both ways)
		Microphone stand
Tools		
	Multiple Head Screwdriver Set	Scissors
	Eyeglass Screwdriver Set	Box Cutter
Miscellaneous		
	Band-Aids	Paper Clips
	Pain Reliever (Aspirin, Acetaminophen)	Rubber Bands
	Antacid tablets	Stapler and Staples
	Table Cover	LED Flashlight
	Kid distractions: Coloring books, crayons, colored pencils	Velcro
Meeting Specific		
	Name Tags	Fliers for Next Meeting
	RSVP List with meeting topic summary printed from Meetup	Promotional Cards or Other Items
Presentations		
	Backup presentation materials, outline	

Ideally, you would want to check the list against the items in the kit before every meeting (at a time and place that you can replace items as needed). Then mark off anything you use up or needs to be discarded during the meeting.

Yes, you can run a successful meeting with few or none of these items...if everything goes according to plan. But I guarantee that if you incorporate the Meeting Toolkit into your meeting preparation, you'll make a lot fewer apologies and have smoother running meetings.

MANAGING YOUR MEMBERS

Many people don't like confrontation. But in nearly every group, there's a person who lives for it or doesn't have the normal social filters we wish everyone used. Sometimes, group members will step up to correct the trouble-maker but in other situations, it just festers. It can cause a whole lot of issues among the group...one ill-behaving person can cause a lot of problems.

The bottom line is this: as the leader, YOU are responsible to a lot of people to create the environment you want. And as leader, you can't blame anyone else for what goes on in the group. You can identify the reasons things happen and are the individual best suited to make changes.

We really want everyone who attends our Meetup group to be comfortable, feel welcome and enjoy the meetings. But there are baseline behaviors that are necessary to provide a home for MOST people. I try to have peer pressure keep people in line, but when it doesn't work, or doesn't work quickly enough, my group is depending on me to do something about it. Members will sometimes come to me because there is an issue but *they* don't want to be the group police. By the time someone comes to me, I know that others are probably having the same reaction and I need to act.

Any time you put people together in a room for a Meetup group, there are a few common issues that may arise.

- **Excessive self-promotion.** This is common with sales people and others who joined your group specifically to get sales leads or sell their services. Everyone else may roll their eyes at these people but when the behavior continues and it is disruptive.

  Don't allow people to use the group as their personal advertising medium to the detriment of others. Doing a *little* self-promotion might be ok, but doing a lot is not. It's a judgment call. And when people step over the line, you help define that line.

- **Unkindness to others.** Ok, unkindness may not be a word, but sometimes it's not bad enough to call it nastiness. It's just general inconsiderate behavior. Some people use the excuse "I'm just being honest," but honesty isn't an excuse for inconsiderate behavior. People always have a choice in how they present their honesty and whether they use it to help or hurt others.

- **Show offs.** We know these people from grade school. They were the ones who needed (and apparently still need) to be first in line and had to show the class that they knew every answer. In doing so, they trample over the feelings of people around them.

- **Nastiness and open hostility.** They may not have an issue with you or your group specifically but they behave in a way that makes everyone cringe. Stem the behavior quickly. Draw focus to something else during the meeting and have a private conversation with them directly after.

In all of these cases, a grand public showing may make you feel that you are showing leadership, but it is not the right solution. Although it may seem well deserved, it approaches the behaviors that the troublemakers are exhibiting. The public confrontation may please a few people but generally leaves most feeling uncomfortable. The best way to show leadership is to show discretion in how it is used.

Instead, approach them *privately* and discuss the observed behaviors and why they disrupt the group (You shouldn't do this *because*...). Give them suggestions for how they can influence the group positively with alternate behaviors.

And ultimately, if nothing else works, you can suggest that they find another group that better suits them. It is within your right to make the decision unilaterally. YOU lead the group.

In the entire history of the Main Line Writers Group, I have only had one person I was forced to ban. Yes, ban. She was rude to people in the critiques of their work. One interesting fact was that her own writing wasn't particularly strong. After several conversations with her and her own inability to moderate her behavior, I suggested that the group was not a match for her and that she should find another group where the match was better. She shot off a group email announcing her mistreatment and a personal email to me offering an opinion on my weaknesses as a leader. I apologized to the group for her behavior and announced that she would no longer be part of the group. If people wanted contact with her, they would need to do that outside of our group.

Only afterwards did I discover that her behavioral problems were the same in several other writers groups and she had been asked to exit from those, as well. Some people just can't make good use of fresh starts, I guess.

I could have made a great public showing, beat my chest and shown the group I was in charge. It would have been a bad move. Years later, she's long forgotten, I am still the leader and people have very positive things to say about how people are treated in the group. So resist the urge to "get even" or "show your Alpha dog superiority" and just let it go.

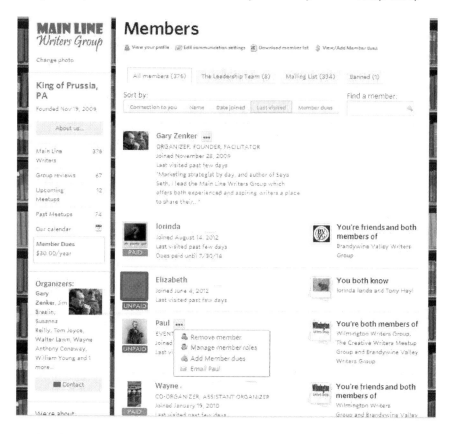

Under the **Members** menu, you can opt to remove individual members. As a leader, consider difficult members as a leadership challenge to help you grow personally. Try to use the **Remove Member** option as a last resort.

There are other uses for the strategy of removing members, including non-payment of dues. What? You haven't implemented dues with your group yet? Or you're not sure you are doing it the right way? That is the perfect segue into...

MONETIZING YOUR GROUP

A STRONG CASE FOR MONETIZATION

Whether or not you organized your group to be a money maker, there are good reasons to monetize your group:

> **It helps to pay back your expenses.** As the leader of a group, you will encounter a variety of expenses, the first of which is the Meetup service itself. Add to that any printing you might do including flyers to attract members in non-electronic fashion or reminders for existing members, handouts, etc. Those sticky backed name tags blanks are expensive and you're printing them for people who show and don't show alike.
>
> You also may need to make token payments to or to pay for the meals of your guest speakers. Maybe you implemented a web site as is suggested earlier in the book and are paying for the hosting fees. Suddenly, you're doing a lot of reaching into your own pocket. And some of those costs can increase as the group becomes more popular.
>
> It all adds up, especially over multiple years. And none of that takes into account the actual time you spend prepping for each meeting.
>
> **It creates an independent valuation for your group.** My very wise grandfather, Sidney Toub, offered this advice to me more than once, "People believe it's worth what it cost them; if you give it away for nothing, that's how they value it." And while that isn't the case for *everything* in life, it is incredibly accurate in general.
>
> People are very susceptible to suggestions regarding value. Even if they doubt something is worth the price being charged, there's a small voice in the back of their heads telling them that

there has to be a logical reason it is priced that way. The higher the price, the higher the perceived value.

There's a joke in marketing: if you can't sell it at the price you have it, double the price and try again. Well, it's not really a joke – it's more of a strategy. And often, it works.

So if you tell people that your meeting is worth $10 or $50, they're likely to believe it at some level. They may not attend, or may not want to pay it, but they're still likely to believe it.

It segregates those with just a casual interest. And the higher the price, the better it performs this function.

Make no mistake: for some people, *any fee* is more than they'll pay. These folks are experts at navigating the system and avoiding payments of any type. Given two choices, even if the pay choice gives them exactly what they want, they choose the freebie.

A fee of any type is the first level of filter and probably the best to eliminate these people from your group.

Why purposefully filter out these people? The fee-resistant individuals have a number of traits that make them more challenging to a group in general:

> *They are the least likely to RSVP YES or NO in advance*, and prone to show up spontaneously, throwing off your attendance counts. For some groups, this can be a problem for the program, or in materials and waste management.
>
> *They are least likely to respect your rules and your leadership*. It's ironic (given the fact that since they are not contributing cash to assist with the group and should be grateful for the "free ride") but this group has the highest personal demands for the group. They tend to be more

disruptive and expect the group to bend to their own individual needs: time, content and ego.

They are most likely to want personal attention through emails and the least likely to follow simple directions. From a leadership standpoint, these members can be time consuming to manage and offer less back to the group as a whole.

They are the first ones to complain about the location, the meal price, etc. Because they are already price-sensitive, if there's no price for attending the group, they fixate on the other areas related to the group that "cost them" money or time.

Their behavior comes from high levels of self-focus: they show low levels of responsibility to the others of the community from the very start.

You can see that if, as a leader, you minimize the distractions of managing difficult people, you can focus more of your time on offering the group improvements in other areas.

SIDE EFFECTS RESULTING FROM MONETIZATION

Sometimes, your efforts in group management create less than desirable side effects, and this is one area where it definitely can. It sometimes results in people very vocally expressing the desire to see where the money is going.

Just to be clear on this subject, you don't owe anyone an explanation of how you spend the funds from the membership unless you really want them to know. Restaurants don't reveal their food and labor costs and training courses don't give you an outline on the costs of running their programs.

I highly recommend that you **do not** give them access to specifics regarding that information. Presenting it opens a can of worms for your operations of the group. Once you start down that route of showing them exactly where the dollars go, they then want to "help you" make the decisions about which expenditures are worthwhile and which are not. It's hard to back away from that once you have started down that road.

YOU are the leader and YOU make the leadership decisions, no matter how democratic a group you run.

When people ask about why there is a membership fee and where the money goes:

1) **Outline the value they receive from the group in general terms.** For the Main Line Writers Group and the Wilmington Writers Group, we offer members a professionally managed monthly meeting where writers can come to a safe, non-judgmental environment to better their craft. They form a support network with people having similar interests and skills. They learn how to better market their own work and avoid problems common to writers.
The group provides presentations on all aspects of writing, group panel discussions on important writing-related topics and an ability to ask specific questions to a group of knowledgeable peers.

   We offer a meeting-friendly, private room with AV capabilities, great acoustics and reasonably-priced meals. We give them an idea of how many hours a month is spent organizing the meetings and taking care of the details.

That should be enough. But if it isn't or you are uncomfortable leaving it at that, you might add this information.

2) **Explain** *in broad terms* **where the money goes**. Without detailing the actual amounts, explain that while Meetup is free to individuals, organizers and leaders pay an ongoing fee to maintain the service. Explain that there are printing and paper costs associated with name tags, handouts, sign-in sheets, promotional cards, etc. Talk about whatever programming costs the group must pay including speaker stipends or meals, etc. Talk about the number of hours that go into planning and running the events for each meeting.

Let's face it, when people walk into a department or specialty store, they don't expect free pants. And they don't expect that the salesperson will outline all of the costs associated with the manufacture and selling of the pants. The store expects to price the item and people will determine for themselves whether the value exceeds or matches the price being asked.

YOU DO NEED TO UNDERSTAND the true value that your group brings to the members and how to put that into words. Let's face it, *anyone* can start and attempt to run a group. Its success depends a great deal on the ability to invest the money and time necessary, and to do the marketing to attract people and the programming to keep it an important value to the attendees. So while the barriers to entry are reasonably low, few people are willing to do what it takes to create a group and then keep it operating to have it become a success. That's why you can charge a membership or meeting fee. And that's exactly why you should charge for your group, as well.

FREE ATTENDANCE TRIAL MEETINGS

That's not to say that you can't or shouldn't offer something for free. Offering a free trial meeting or a low cost intro meeting can be a very effective and important marketing approach for your group. After all, most people (probably yourself included) don't want to pay for things that they aren't sure about and they surely don't want to buy a membership in something that they haven't tried. A trial meeting offers them a sample taste of your group. If your value proposition is a good one, most people will opt in for the membership fee.

MONETIZATION OPTIONS

Ok, now that you've decided that you are comfortable with the concept of monetizing the group (if you aren't, go back and read the previous passage again), the next question is *HOW to do it*? An annual membership fee? A per-meeting fee? Both? Something else? This really depends on the group itself, the frequency of meetings, the content and dynamics of the group, your costs involved, your goals, the people you are likely to attract and the value that the group offers.

Whew. That's a lot to consider. So let's look at some of your options and the implications that surround them.

> **Annual fees.** Annual fees offer specific advantages and a few disadvantages. Collecting a lump sum up front means that you have funds for a person's attendance whether they show up to one meeting or all of them. That's very desirable from a financial management standpoint!
>
> Collecting money from individuals up front also has the desirable effect of motivating people to actually show up to meetings. Most people, if they've pre-paid to attend something, are more committed to attending than if they didn't. It means that advance payments can boost your attendance, which will in turn attract others because the group has higher attendance: a self-fulfilling prophecy.
>
> **The downside to annual fees** is that the people who pay them and don't end up attending are unlikely to renew after their

membership expires. After all, everyone who pays an annual membership fee has good intentions. They do it expecting to show up to most or all of the meetings. Then life gets in the way. At the end of their year, they may do some mental calculations and figure out how much each attended meeting cost them.

And while the cost per meeting may still be reasonable, they'll realize that they spent three to six times as much per meeting than they intended. And that's where buyer's remorse kicks in. They thought they were paying $3 a meeting but they actually paid $12. Even if the meeting was worth $12 (hell, most people pay more than that for a modest priced dinner out), it isn't what they EXPECTED to have paid per meeting. They have negative feelings even though they themselves controlled their attendance. So they don't think about that, and sometimes they don't even think about how they could attend more meetings next year.

So the fact that you got a membership fee from them the one time is exactly why you may not get it the second time.

Does that mean that the annual membership is a bad idea? NO. It only means that for some people, if you don't have a pay-per-meeting option, you'll lose them after the first annual fee.

And as we've covered, you do get something more than money up front from an annual membership fee. You get motivation to attend and that is important. If your group is like so many others, participation is one of the strongest motivators for people to come back and others to pay their annual membership fee to join in the first place. Who wants to join and attend a small, inactive group?

Pay per meeting. Charging for individual meetings also offers certain advantages and, as you would expect, some disadvantages. A per-meeting fee offers members the ability to begin attending your meetings without the theoretical time commitment that a membership fee might imply. They don't have to think about their schedule for the next twelve months; they only have to worry about one thing: *will I have time to make the meeting I am trying to schedule?* That is a much easier decision to make.

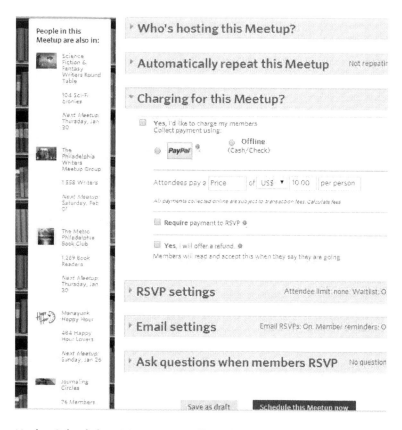

Under **Schedule a Meetup**, scrolling down shows you the option to set up a pay-per-meeting fee.

There's also a financial aspect from the member standpoint. Individuals who may have been reluctant to plunk down a single larger payment for the annual fee are more willing to pay the more nominal per-meeting fee. It's an easier decision to pay $10 for a meeting instead of $55 for a year's worth of meetings.

That's because people in general won't aggregate the year's worth of payments in their heads and calculate the total they are paying for one if they attend all the meetings. In their minds, it's a one-time payment for a one-time benefit, even if it recurs every month.

The downside to pay per meeting. Per-meeting fees don't have the same attendance motivation that annual fees hold. Because payment is on an a la carte basis, people don't have a self-imposed financial motivation to attend, pushed by the money they have already spent.

You will also have different cash flow resulting. Theoretically, if you have a constant flow of new and returning members to your groups, your cash flow could be equivalent or higher, as people return and pay their attendance fees monthly.

You will, however, need to factor in that people may attend fewer meetings for a fee-per-meeting structure. If you run an unpopular program, attendance goes down and the potential income with it; if circumstances like weather force you to cancel a meeting, income is completely lost. With an annual fee, the session has already been covered by the membership fee (albeit at perhaps a lower fee).

With so many variables involved, there's no exact equation you can apply to figure which approach will pay off better for your group. The best thing you can do is look at the nature of *your* group, consider the members and their original motivations for attending, and try to understand the value received from the member side. Those factors will guide you as to what fee approach makes the most sense. Or maybe, you should really consider a hybrid...

Annual membership OR per meeting fee. Sometimes, **combining** the payment options in some way is a reasonable solution, such as offering an either/or option: pay a membership or pay a meeting fee. Offering a hybrid combination addresses a few of the weaknesses in the individual methods.

Advantages for membership:

- People will feel that they have more choice in what they pay (most people like choices).
- It clearly establishes a higher (and probably more motivating) value for the individual meetings by placing a price tag on attending that way.
- People who mentally compare the cost of single meeting vs. membership attendance will see a stronger value for the membership (assuming that your annual membership cost is less than twelve times the cost of attending individual meetings). You can even offer them this comparison directly to emphasize the savings.
- People who have opted for membership and had absences will feel that they have another option as opposed to renewing a membership they won't fully use.

Advantages for leadership:

- You are less likely to lose members entirely when they have more, varied payment options.

Unfortunately, offering this also adds complication to the tracking process for meeting payments and memberships.

Tracking membership is easy: print the member list before the meeting. If they aren't listed as a member and it isn't their sample meeting, they are not members and don't get the meeting as part of their membership. That's simple.

Tracking the per-meeting fee is easy: print the RSVP list with payments. If they show up without having paid in advance, they haven't paid for the attendance with a per-meeting fee. Also very simple.

Tracking both as payment options and combining them to see whether members have done one or the other requires a bit more work and comparing a few print-outs, but it may offer a great solution for your group.

The challenge with this hybrid approach is that if you want to do your tracking through Meetup (and I highly recommend that you do in all situations possible), the system does not offer a practical way to manage all of it for you in a single report.

Yes, you can track memberships. Yes, you can arrange for attendees to pay a meeting fee. You can even do both independently of each other (meaning you can track them doing both, albeit as separate functions). But the system doesn't give people a choice of one OR the other as online payment for the meeting.

A WORKAROUND FOR OFFERING
MEMBERSHIP OR PER-PAY MEETING FEE OPTION

There is a workaround, but it involves a bit of manual work (using a couple of Meetup's standard reports), which may be more administration than you care to do. Here's the work-around:

- Select the **Members** pull-down menu at the top of the screen

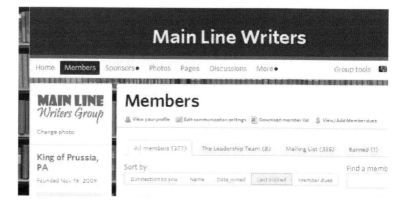

Click on Download member list and open the file with EXCEL or a compatible program.

You will have a spreadsheet with a lot of extraneous data that will look something like this:

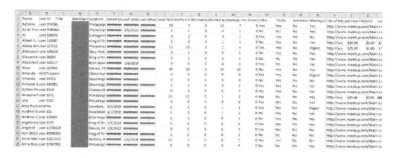

You will need to use this sheet to track the event for the evening and want to bring it with you for non-RSVP attendees. That necessitates that you make it more manageable (my group list spans 350+ entries long and nearly 26 columns wide as downloaded...yours may be shorter).

To print the sheet:

- Click the top left corner so that the entire spreadsheet is highlighted and change the font to Arial Narrow 10 point type. More type fits in the same space this way.
- The headline row should be bold

- Hide the data columns not needed for tracking the meeting payments. That means you should hide columns B, C, D, E, F, H, I, J, K, L, M, N, O, P, Q, R, S, U by selecting these columns and selecting the **HIDE COLUMN** option under the pull-down menu
- Change the header to minimize column widths
    - Change header F to read **Join Date**
    - Change header G to read **Last Attend**
    - Change header S to read **Last Pmt**
    - Change header U to read **Last Pmt Dt**
- Adjust column widths to correctly fit the data
- This is your complete Member and Annual Fee list

	A	F	G	S	T	U
1	Name	Join Date	Last Attend	Last PMT	Refund	Last Pmt Dt
2		8/30/2010	1/16/2013			
3		9/17/2012	9/19/2012			
4		12/31/2010	9/19/2012			
5		8/15/2013	10/16/2013	$30.00	$0.00	8/1/2013
6		11/28/2011	12/18/2013	$25.00	$0.00	1/7/2013
7		6/18/2012	1/16/2013			
8		6/18/2013	6/19/2013			
9		3/21/2011				
10		6/23/2010	1/15/2014			
11		3/20/2012				
12		1/12/2012				
13		5/23/2013	6/19/2013			
14		2/23/2013				
15		10/27/2013	1/15/2014	$30.00	$0.00	12/27/2013
16		11/23/2013				
17		8/3/2010	9/22/2010			
18		2/7/2010	4/21/2010			
19		7/15/2010	1/18/2012			
20		1/1/2013	1/15/2014			
21		2/8/2012				
22		4/12/2013	4/17/2013			
23		12/11/2011	6/20/2012			
24		7/19/2011	8/15/2012			
25		7/19/2012	8/15/2012			
26		5/2/2011	5/26/2011			
27		11/25/2012				
28		12/27/2012				

Ah! Much easier to manage. Now you have a list of members showing which ones paid their membership fees. Your member names as they appear in Meetup will appear in the Name column....I have blocked them in the example for privacy purposes. Now go to your current meeting that you need to track.

Add a column between S and T and name it "Meet fee 00/00/00" where you insert the date of the meeting in place of the 00/00/00.

Now you need to download the list of members who have RSVP'd and paid for the meeting on a per-meeting basis and append the spreadsheet. To do this:

- Click on the meeting you are seeking to track
- Open the tools menu to the right and select Download RSVP

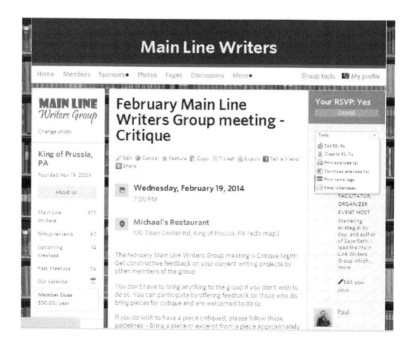

- Download it, then open the spreadsheet. Match the RSVP names to the master membership list previously downloaded.
- Print that sheet out and bring it to your meeting. You will need to repeat this process every meeting because paid memberships will change - you will have new members and some memberships will expire and not be renewed.

Also note that you will probably have stragglers who did not RSVP at all but do show up to the meeting; you will need to compare them to the Membership list.

Will stragglers lie to you and say that they RSVPd and paid when they haven't? I hope not, but be prepared. Either bring a device with you that you can check their status on site or put right in the meeting directions that RSVPs after a certain date and time can only be paid at the meeting. This is a common approach.

CHARGING *BOTH* MEMBERSHIP AND PER-MEETING FEES

Tracking is actually easier when you charge **both** a membership fee AND a meeting fee. That's because you assume that **everyone** needs to be a member of the group (maybe after the free sample meeting) and the meeting fee is independent of that fact. Everyone also needs to pay the per-meeting fee for the RSVP.

You follow the same steps in creating a modified membership list and then appending it with the information on the RSVPs from the meeting.

The system has the ability to require the meeting charge to be paid online at the time of RSVP. The positive is that it simplifies things and your tracking is done automatically. The negative is that it may inhibit some people from placing their RSVP early, knowing that they will be charged the minute they RSVP. That may give your meetings a very delayed RSVP response.

Should you charge both fees? *Can* you charge both? Again, there's no easy answer to these questions but the questions are worthy of consideration. You have to look both at your needs as a group leader and those of the members who receive a value from the group.

As a leader, you might choose to charge both as a way to have a lower membership fee while still achieving a financial goal of having money paid up-front. The membership fee may help eliminate some of the high maintenance-low involvement members we examined earlier. Mixing a per-meeting fee on top of that may offset specific meeting costs and help you establish a value of the meetings themselves, beyond the group.

But think like a member, who is likely to ask "why should I pay twice to be a member of a group?" so be prepared with a reasonable answer. That answer involves the fact that they are not paying twice, they are paying in two parts. But that is harder to understand when they are indeed paying more than once.

USE THE MEETUP.COM PAYMENT SYSTEM

MeetUp offers a membership tracking function and allows payments to be made by members online. Whether you opt to charge for memberships or for individual meetings (either or both), you should use and promote the online payment system actively.

Here's why: as soon as someone is willing to pay for the meeting or the membership, you want to make it easy for them to do that. You don't want them to second guess or delay. Collecting at the actual meeting should be a last resort if possible. And honestly, if they pay online, you have a lot less manual tracking to do (more on that a bit further in the text).

Our groups find people fairly split on how they pay. About half opt for payment in person and half online. Some are moved to pay as the system sends out automated messages telling them that their membership is due (a nice feature that takes me personally off the hook for sending out notices manually or mentioning it on every email). The fact that people will pay it online is a great reason to offer that feature.

Fees for collecting the fees. The online system charges a fee for the collection of membership fees that comes out of the collected fees. You receive the net of the membership fee minus the processing fee. I don't agonize over the percentage they take...I just 'mark up' the membership fee to cover the processing cost.

Setting up online fee collection: setting the type of collection you want. To set your membership fee:

- Go to the **Group Tools** pull-down menu and select **MONEY**.
- Choose **Manage Member Dues**.
- You'll be presented with a number of options, including the ability to charge an annual or monthly membership fee (this is different than a meeting fee) and to offer information on what the fees are used for.

You can make fees required before RSVPing for an event (**TO ATTEND**), required before joining the online group (**TO BE A MEMBER** after a designated trial period) or optional (**IF THEY WANT**). Keep in mind that the free trial length is related to timing after signing up online, and has nothing to do with actual meeting attendance. Since the system removes people from the group after the trial period ends if they don't pay the membership fee, you could give them 60 days and they just don't get around to showing up in that time. That would eliminate them from the group before they even attended a meeting.

Obviously, this option works well for groups where people are motivated to show up immediately, but not as well if they don't and you want to try motivating them to show up over a longer period of time.

I personally feel that if they don't want to stop the notices coming, then I want to keep sending them.

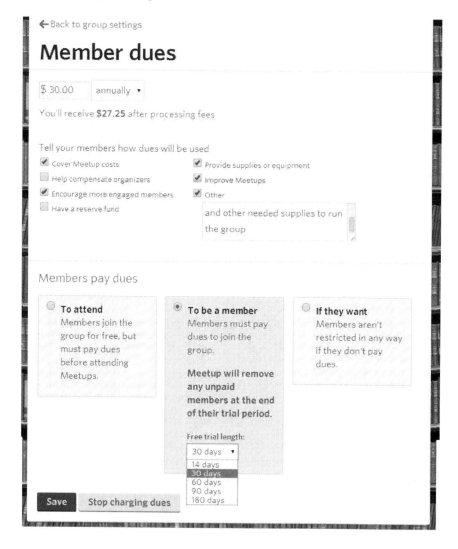

To review payments made through the group:

- Go to the **Group Tools** pull-down menu

- Select the **Money** option.
- Scroll down until you reach **All Transactions** and you can see the payments made in latest-first order.

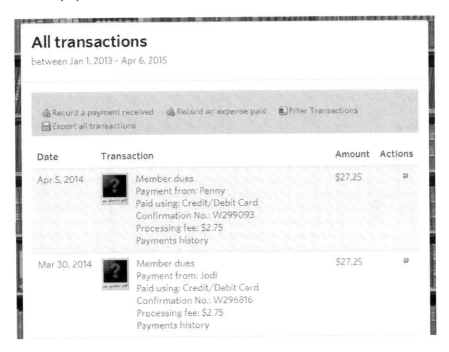

You can also view members grouped by those who have and those who have not made payments by selecting the Members pull-down menu and selecting the **Member Dues** tab. Current paid members are listed first, followed by non-current members (again, specific data in this example is blocked for privacy).

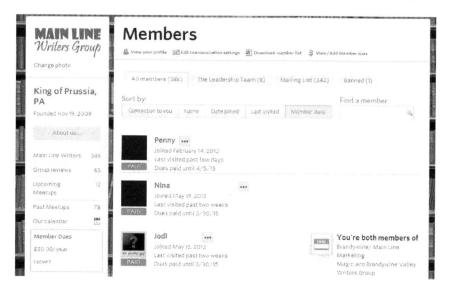

Payments made outside the online system. If you allow payments to be made by check or cash during the meetings, your online tracking can easily accommodate those payments and merge the tracking with ones made through the system. At any time, you can go into any member profile and manually add their membership or meeting payment.

To do this, go to the Members screen and select Add members dues

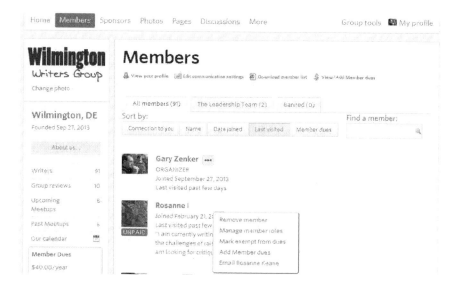

Then enter the data you want to record

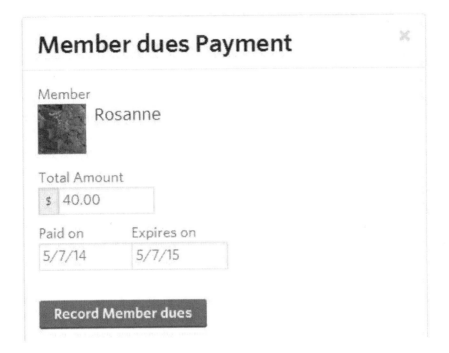

Creating non-standard and complementary memberships. You may want people that you want to appear as members but pay a different fee or no fee at all. You can accomplish that as well. When you go in to add membership, just change the dollars to what you want them to be (or even $0) and set the start and end date for the membership. This option works for a variety of situations, including:

- Short-term trial memberships
- Complimentary memberships for presenters or leaders
- If you want to institute a premium membership of some type

Setting up online fee collection: you need an account. You need two accounts to accept payments:

- An online processing account to which the member money gets initially placed
- a checking account to which it is eventually transferred.

To set up the processing account (Meetup uses WePay), you will need your checking account number and the **bank routing number** (a nine number generally on the bottom left of your checks.

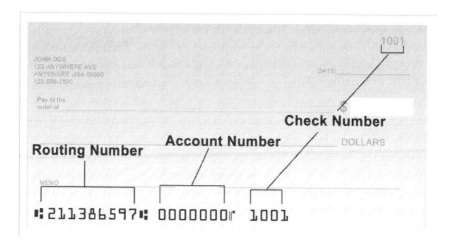

To set up your processing account:

- Go to **Settings** under your personal account information in Meetup and choose **Payments Received** from the sidebar menu.
- Scroll down and follow the prompts to set up your **WePay** account.
- You can also use your existing PayPal account and enter that information, as well.

Your WePay account

Manage your WePay account

Your PayPal account

PayPal is a 3rd-party website that allows you to collect money securely online.

You are currently set up to receive money with PayPal.

- Collect dues for your Meetup Groups
- Charge members to attend your meetup events

Enter the email address you use for PayPal to link your accounts

Your members will be able to see this email address

Save PayPal Information

Note that the email you use for your PayPal account will be shown to any Meetup member who sends you a payment using PayPal.

Learn more about how Meetup works with PayPal

Set up a separate checking account for electronic payments. On the surface, it seems unnecessary to go through the effort of setting up a completely new bank account just for Meetup payments, but there are very good reasons to do so. One involves tracking; the others involves protection.

> *Tracking:* By having an account with only the money from the group coming in and going out, it's easier to segregate the funds and track both individual and aggregate transactions. Sure, you could do it with your personal account but then you have irrelevant transactions mixed in with the groups. Going back later to examine the records is a pain in the...neck.

> *Protection:* As the leader of the group, you will probably be responsible for the financial aspects of the group. But you may

have someone helping you. Having separate accounts limits access that extra person has to just the money in that one account. It denies them access to your other personal or business funds.

And there's another form of protection that is very important – protection from the payment system itself.

An important warning about payment systems. When you sign up to accept deposits from pay systems (**PayPal, We Pay**, etc), you will sign a whole lot of disclosure which generally comes down to this: they are the final arbitrator in all things regarding the payments received and the goods or services you are selling. If someone who paid you complains they didn't get the value or services promised, they can initiate an action to take that money back. That money can be "sucked" back out of your account and the pay system is the final arbitrator. And they can do it at nearly any time.

How could that go wrong for you? Suppose you are running low on funds one month, and expect to use the existing funds from your PayPal account. Then a couple of people create a payment dispute, and the system sucks the money in dispute out of your account. They don't tell you ahead of time, it's just withdrawn. Then there isn't enough in your personal account to pay your mortgage or other incoming checks or e-bills. You could end up with bounced check charges. Maybe lots of them. Co-mingling your personal accounts with the group funds could cost you hundreds of dollars in bank fees.

That example alone should be enough reason for you to segregate your group funds from your personal funds. The good news is that some banks still offer a zero or low minimum balance checking account. You can set it up for electronic transfers to your primary personal (or business) account and never need to pay for physical checks.

Meetup is a valuable tool in organizing the resources you need to conduct impactful and memorable meetings. From group organization and member involvement to monetization and marketing, it handles many of the group management tasks and integrates them for you.

LEVERAGING YOUR SUCCESS

However you measure your success (remember back to the beginning of this book?) your goals and subsequent achievements can help guide and shape *your next efforts* within and even outside the group.

Start by thinking carefully about your goals and achievements related to the group. The best way to really assess them is to write them down.

GOALS, ACHIEVEMENTS, AND BENEFITS EXERCISE

You may have some goals that don't have a related achievement, and you may have some achievements not tied to specific goals. That's fine, we're not judging, but rather, we are taking an inventory.

There are two sets of intersecting goals and achievements we want to record here: goals and achievements *for the group*, and goals and achievements *for you as an individual and leader of the group.*

Let's start by getting them down in written (or typed) form.

GROUP

GOALS	ACHIEVEMENTS	BENEFIT

LEADER

GOALS	ACHIEVEMENTS	BENEFIT

If you're like most leaders, you've probably achieved a lot more than you realize. Looking at your goals, achievements and the benefits gained both individually and in aggregate will often reveal patterns or opportunities for future potential.

This is a great opportunity to have some other people in the group help you list these important elements. You may be too modest, or just not see some of the greatness you and your group have achieved. Don't be shy or think that your members believe that you are seeking a pat on the back. This step can be crucial in your group's growth and your own personal growth.

Some Examples: Achievements/Benefits to the Group

For help with Goals, you can go back to your original list that you created at the beginning of this book and add any that you have identified since.

This list of common achievements may help you identify some of your own group's successes:

- Large group of online members

- Regular schedule of meetings over xx months
- Active meetings
- # core active members
- # average meeting attendance
- Hosted excellent programs
- Completed specific projects (identify)
- Provided specific training (identify)

To help broaden your thinking, let's use the example of the achievements and benefits of the Main Line Writers.

Achievement / Benefit 1 – Created sub-groups and held extra meetings to provide additional member education opportunities. We used the surveys to test additional offerings from the group which resulted in offering a bi-monthly, specialized critique (writing review session). It was limited to ten attendees on a first-come, first served basis. One of the very talented members had a passion for leading it, so we let him run everything related to it. That is, I gave him administrator access to the site to set his own meetings and let him manage the whole thing. He selects the timing and the location of the meeting. It became a monthly meeting with a core group and a couple of spots where different people came in and out of the meeting.

It later morphed from 10 people reading a 25 page excerpt from each participant to the entire group focusing on one 250 page piece from one writer each meeting. There isn't any other place locally where writers can get ten people to focus on and critique that large a work, which adds a completely new value to the group.

This was a tremendous win in a number of ways. The group overall benefitted from the offering. The leader of the critique has a sense of pride and ownership for the group without unnecessary interference from someone who doesn't even attend the meeting. I personally look like I offer the group more benefits for their success. Win-win-win.

Achievement / Benefit 2 – Published a print volume and e-book to create additional exposure for authors as writers and learn needed skills related to marketing and publishing. Four years in, we asked ourselves what next expansion effort would benefit the members the most? For writers, being published is obviously a big achievement (being paid is, of course, an even bigger one). So I started thinking about how we could make that happen.

The core membership agreed that publishing a book of short stories with specific guidelines would be a great project. It would not only give members a publishing venue but it would allow us all to go through the publishing process and learn from it about start to finish.

Without going into irrelevant details, nine months later we are one of the few Meetup writers groups nationwide to have published a collection of work by our members. With one of the requirements for work submission being a paid up membership, we drove some additional operating funds to the group and deeper involvement from a number of people including members not having representation in the book. And we have the membership asking if and when we will be publishing the next collection.

Achievement / Benefit 3: Add a completely new type of monthly programming to the group.

The one type of programming that the group never offered in the first five years of operation involved actual writing. On the surface that may sound strange, but writers are a funny lot. Most of them labor in isolation while working their craft. And many will only show their work after they make dozens of revisions.

Writing and sharing on the spot means that you have to write short pieces or segments and you don't have the time to polish. I was concerned that kind of pressure would alienate most of the group. But offering a single session as a trial on a day separate from the regular monthly meeting, we received 33 RSVPs in less than 24 hours, a full month prior to the session! That was an unprecedented response from the group and a clear indication of the kind of programming they want.

And suddenly, we have a second monthly meeting covering a very specific topic.

Achievement / Benefit 4: Built an entirely new writers group to expand the reach and influence with the writers of the area and have a network of groups that work together to offer resources and education.

As I listened to the reasons people did and did not show up to the Main Line Writers Group meetings, geography was an issue. We have some people travel an hour and a half to come to our group. But some don't do it regularly and others offered the feedback we were just too far from them geographically. After visually surveying the groups publicized on Meetup, I saw an opportunity to locate a new group 40 minutes south of the existing group.

This opportunity wasn't because no other groups existed; I found a number of existing groups. But as I dug deeper, I discovered that some seemed stagnant (no meetings in the last four months) and none of them offered the combination of education, writing feedback and fellowship that our group did.

The new group had the potential to start from a strong foundation. There were a few people that I knew would show up on a regular basis (they would switch from one group to the other). That also meant that they already knew each other and would form a good core. I also had experience with the programming. Some of my previous presenters would fit easily into the new group schedule.

I expected ten people to show up at the first meeting (about the number of the other group when I started); twenty showed up. And twenty signed up for the second meeting. A strong showing and a great place to start building another success.

But why an entirely new group? We could have created additional meetings for the existing writers group in a different geographic location and attempt to build the one group larger. I made a conscious decision NOT to go that route. Although the name of the group was inherited, the title Main Line Writers offered geographic boundaries, appropriate for the original and subsequent meeting places we selected. It has no significance when creating a meeting group across state lines into Delaware.

By creating a new group with a new name, existing or new members didn't feel that they were missing any part of the group's programming, nor did outside presenters feel that they were repeating the same programming for the same group. They were perfectly willing, however, to offer the same programming to two different groups even though they were run by the same leader.

It also gave the group the ability to raise its own membership funds and be priced differently, given what was learned from the Main Line Writers Group.

There are more achievements and benefits, of course, but these should give you an idea of how to begin framing your thinking on this topic.

Some Examples: Achievements / Benefits to you as a leader

A successfully managed group and satisfied members can also lead to a number of *personal* benefits besides a filling of all your waking hours with additional work. The Meetup can lead to personal benefits including reputation enhancement, learning additional skill sets, and even income opportunities.

To help you fill in your own list of achievements and benefits, consider whether these achievements match your own in leading the group:

- New learned skills (list them individually)
- Improved leadership skills
- Involvement in a particular discipline
- Reputation building in areas (list them)
- Networking with recognized experts in specific areas
- General networking with other professionals

Once again, to broaden your thinking and give you some ideas how these may apply to you, consider these specific examples for our situation:

Achievement / Benefit 1: Professional reputation enhancement.

Written feedback on the Meetup site in addition to endorsements and written recommendations on Linkedin, offer me reputation-enhancing feedback in the areas of leadership, written communications and a variety of marketing-related categories.

Your own hard work managing your group should lead to personal and professional recommendations and endorsements. In the pre-Internet days, this might have taken the form of letters of recommendation. Today's environment offers a much more efficient and effective method of recognition through social media.

Ironically, the same challenges exist today that have always existed: you generally need to **ask** for the endorsements and recommendations. While the media has changed greatly, people have not. Some people would be happy to offer you the public feedback but they will never think about doing it unless you ask. Others will do it eventually but you'll have to ask several times before they place it on their priority list. The rest won't do it because they themselves are not involved in the appropriate social media or they just aren't comfortable with that sort of thing.

If you use LinkedIn, you know that it can be hard to build your reputation there. Some companies have rules against their employees offering public recommendations and endorsements. Some of the people who would offer the best feedback are not involved or just can't be pushed to do it for you. Your Meetup group offers a new list of people who may be more motivated to help.

So, focus on the ones who will and forget about the others. Don't feel hurt or question why they wouldn't do it for you. You will only waste a lot of time and effort on something you can't change.

Achievement / Benefit 2: Business Opportunity: Self-Publishing Education and Programming. The creation of the Main Line Writers Group book drove another realization: authors were unprepared for the multitude of tasks and efforts related to self-publishing. A small subset of the membership did the work on the group's book, but except for me, no one had their hand in ALL of the tasks. The work on formatting and creating the file for publishing was a solo task. Their knowledge of social media was not advanced enough to be of much help. None understood the needs of marketing the book.

In the meantime, I used my knowledge gained to publish 9 additional books (including this one) which continue to be available through Amazon.com. That work reinforced my skill and expertise in the details of producing and marketing books. My entrepreneurial background helped guide me to set up my own publishing company.

Achievement / Benefit 3: Coaching and Consulting Role. Using all that knowledge, I began to develop a separate, comprehensive program to guide authors from concept to the marketing of their work. I coached individual authors on their efforts to self-publish and even acted as full press agent for an author referred to me for that purpose.

My time spent managing the group returned additional income, valuable experience, and credibility in an area of marketing I previously had not explored.

Again, these are just examples. Think through your own situation.

NOW, LEVERAGE IT ALL

So now you're starting to really think about all the benefits you have gained from running the group. Next, use the previous examples to think about some of the possibilities YOU have.

First things first: connect with others. Two of the most useful social media vehicles are Linkedin and Facebook. Hopefully, you already have accounts tied to you personally and professionally. So start by seeking out every person in your group and connect with them through these vehicles. In both of these forums, they need to be connected with you to take the next step in endorsements or recommendations.

Next, ask for their help. While it would be really nice for people to spontaneously do this for you, the fact is that for most people to actually do it, you will need to ask them for their help. Ask them as a group at the close of your in-person meetings and as individuals in e-mail communications. Use judgment so that it isn't part of every communication, but keep in mind that many people will need follow-ups and reminders.

In your communications, explain why it is important to you. It's one thing to ask people to help you, but it's more effective when you tell them why it is important (remember the power of "because...") Explain that the recommendation is a very personal "Thank you" for the time and effort you spend managing the group and arranging for the events or programs that benefit each and every one of the members.

You won't score anywhere near 100% in your response. But the people who do it may surprise you with the things they say. And having those comments online, associated with their profiles is a strong positive for you, no matter where you go next.

Make it easier for them: offer them guidance. *LinkedIn* is the most valuable repository for the endorsements and recommendations. That's because the people reading your profile know that the person credited actually published the quote and can reference *their* professional background. That offers great credibility built into the system.

Your challenge is the structure of Linked in and the fact that most people don't know how to write a decent recommendation. You need to show them how to write their recommendations.

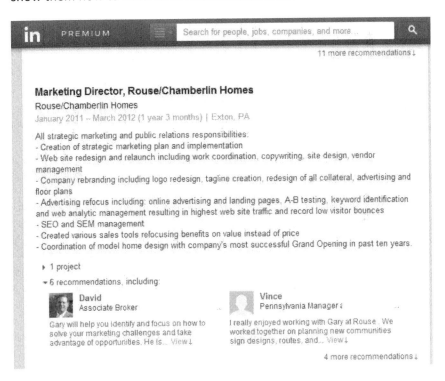

Linked In shows only the first couple of lines of a recommendation and requires that the viewer click to expand the quote to read its full content. The result of people writing without direction is often a quote that may not make sense or takes too long to get to the point.

You get a much better quote by teaching them how to write the quote using an example.

When I request a recommendation through an email, I ALWAYS include a well-structured example and explain why it is best in that format. People will sometimes use what I give them almost exactly, but most of the time they customize it. Supplying it that way also allows me to make suggestions as to relevant points instead of leaving it completely up to them. That gives me a bit more control on what they might say.

Here's one example of an email you could use:

Dear {Name}

Thanks for being a part of the {group name}. I work hard to ensure that every meeting is relevant and worth your time investment. I could use your help in two ways.

Offer your feelings on the group and its leadership on Meetup.
People choose the group based on the group description and the written reviews of the group and meetings. Take the opportunity to write something positive about the group on our group Meetup site. Go to *www.Meetup.com/groupname,* and enter a comment for the group itself and for events. Entering something about every meeting you attend would be awesome.

Offer *a personal recommendation for me on Linkedin.* This would be an amazing recognition of the efforts I make personally and it helps me professionally. You can do this by logging onto your own existing Linkedin account, connecting with me if you are not already connected, and doing these two things:

1. **Offer endorsements.** Go to my profile and scroll down to **Skills and Endorsements**. Simply click to endorse me for any

and all skills that you believe are accurate for me (I hope there's a lot!) Don't forget LEADERSHIP!

2. **Create a written recommendation.** These are most important as they give you a chance to really customize what you want to say about me.

- Go to the blue **Send a Message** button, click the arrow on the side and select **Recommendation**.
- Choose a category. Many group members select Business Partner
- Make selections from the pull-down options and type a written recommendation on what you think about my various skills you see in action as leader of the {group name}. The best written recommendations are structured with an introductory summary and a concluding summary, sandwiching details behind your recommendation. It might read something like this:

> "Gary is an outstanding leader. His hard work and preparation for the Main Line Writers Group offers a community resource that is professional, well-planned out and vital to people at all levels of writing. For over five years, Gary has been committed to the group and the core goals of education, self-improvement and an environment of sharing. This is the best writers group I have ever attended. "

> PLEASE use your own words. I appreciate your willingness to do this for me.

> Thank you!

Detailed instructions like these will get you the best results. In particular, you want that brief complete compliment in the first line.

LEAVING YOUR GROUP

Given your passion that drove you to run the group, it might be hard to imagine a reason for leaving your group behind. But the need for your departure can arise unexpectedly. You may have a geographic move that makes managing or attending the group impossible. You may have new responsibilities in other parts of your life that make it impractical to run it the way you feel it should be run. Or it may turn out that you just don't have the member attendance necessary to make it worth your time and resource investment.

At this point, you have a couple of choices: turn the leadership over to someone else, close it down or just let it fade.

Letting it fade is the easiest option. Just do nothing. Set no meetings, abandon all communications and when the money comes due for the Meetup renewal, don't authorize it.

I really hope you won't select this option. The challenge with this approach is that, as long as the group is still an official group, people can opt to join. As the leader, people see your name associated with a stagnant group. With no meetings set and no response to the messages sent to you, people make assumptions about you personally. That probably isn't really what you want and those assumptions may be grossly unfair. And it really isn't fair or respectful to the people who expressed interest in your group.

Turning the leadership over to someone else does involve some work. You'll need to find someone appropriate, help them understand the nature of the group more deeply, turn over your resources, change site administrator status, etc. Presumably, you want to leave the new leader with the best chance for ongoing success. Taking all of these steps is the best and most responsible thing you can do for your group and its membership.

Planning is the key to any successful change in leadership. A great approach would be to solicit interest in new leadership BEFORE pulling yourself out of Meetup sponsorship. While Meetup will automatically send notices to the group members seeking a replacement leader when you withdraw your leadership, what you have really done in that case is abandoned the group. Maybe the group never met your expectations or the members weren't the type you hoped to attract. But a little bit of effort to explain your departure to the group and to find a replacement leader is the classy way of saying "Hello. I must be going."

There's no guarantee that the person who takes it over will care as much as you did, or that they will run the group in the same way or with the same goals and values you did. But if you are giving up the leadership, you give up that control as well.

Finding the replacement leader is an attempt to offer a legacy. Maybe the group grows into one that hosts hundreds of people at each meeting. You'll know that you were a large part of that success by actively passing the group leadership to the next person. And from a selfish standpoint, how impressive is it if you started a group that lasts five or ten years and hosts hundreds of people? You get credit for some of that even if you aren't currently running the group. Maybe you get an honorary membership or your photo in a permanent place on the group's MeetUp page.

Sometimes, the change can result in success for the group overall. The Main Line Writers Group is a great example of what can happen with positive changes in leadership.

An individual had set up the structure and a total of 14 people were interested enough to join the online group. The then-leader had trouble setting up an actual in-person meeting. She cancelled once, set up another meeting and then suddenly cancelled the meeting *two hours before* it was supposed to happen. When I received the email, I wondered about all the people who wouldn't see the email, would show up at the meeting site and be disappointed. So I wrote her a fast note offering that observation and that maybe someone should be there to explain the meeting was cancelled. And as long as someone would be there, maybe it could be an informal chat opportunity.

She wasn't at all happy with my comments. She told me that I had overstepped my boundaries and was quite rude to me (maybe not a surprise given she took no one else's feelings into consideration cancelling a meeting two hours prior to its scheduled start). At that moment, I remember swearing that I would never attend a meeting of *her group*. Two days later she abandoned the group as a notice went out to all members stating that she was no longer the leader. I can only assume that a few other people offered similar observations that were also not welcomed.

I took on the leadership role, thinking that if 14 people wanted to meet, I could make that happen. Two months later we had our first meeting (in a different location which was more amenable to a discussion group). The biggest compliments I received that day were that it was "very well organized" and "it was more democratic" than the attendees expected it to be. These were two of the nicest compliments possible for me.

Five years later, The Main Line Writers Group is going strong and has grown into something no one could have imagined then. The group has one of the largest local memberships for writers groups outside the city of Philadelphia. We have ongoing attendance of 26-45 people at every meeting.

The group has done things no other local group has attempted: in October 2013, the group published a collection of stories by group members. In May 2014 we will start a multi-member blog designed to help members gain a new audience for their writing. Also in May 2014 we started a second monthly meeting with the focus specifically on writing (as opposed to presentations on writing-related topics). We've spoken about publishing a second book. Pretty damn good for a group that was abandoned by the previous leader before the first meeting ever happened.

The point here is that a change in leadership led the group to regular organized meetings and ongoing growth, the best possible outcome. If you need to leave the group, give your group a chance to survive and thrive: seek out an interested leader.

When closing the group down is the only practical option. In some cases, it happens: you have no one interested in taking over the leadership (which, remember, requires that person to be responsible for the Meetup fee to start). Without a leader to manage the Meetup site, schedule and lead meetings, etc., there is no group.

Rather than leave it abandoned on Meetup, communicate with everyone who is already a member. Change the greeting for the group. Close the group to new members joining. Search and see if there is another group that might fit your members' needs. Contact the leader of that group and merge with them. Then close your group down completely.

Yes, it does take another hour or two to take all these extra steps. But it's the right thing to do. It shows character and respect.

FINAL THOUGHTS

There isn't a meeting that goes by that *someone* doesn't come up to me, as leader of the group, and tell me how grateful they are for our group and my leadership in running it. I think I can say without exaggeration that I have changed some people's lives. Maybe just a little, but I've given them opportunities to make new friends and increase their self-confidence, offered them a place to learn about their craft and presented new interests. Come to think of it, maybe that shouldn't be described as just a "little." That is an amazing thing to be able to do for others. I consider myself lucky and privileged to be in the position and have the skills to help so many people.

And if that isn't enough to justify doing it, in leading the groups I've also grown personally. I've met incredible talent and have a whole new list of friends who I care about and who care about me beyond the group itself. I've extended my social network outside the group using the members as leverage for that. I've discovered interests and talents I didn't realize that reside within me. I've learned subject matter, become smarter and extended my ability to solve new challenges. So if helping other people isn't a good enough reason to do it and continue to do it, I've made real personal gains as well.

My hope is that this book offers some guidance to make your own efforts pay off even better for both your group members and for you personally. And I would love to hear about your achievements as a result of the information in this book. Please email me at garyzenker@gmail.com and let me know what you thought about the book and/or how it made a difference for you or your group.

Your leadership can make a huge difference to a lot of other people. I hope that you take the responsibility seriously and use it to help others.

APPENDIX A - PUBLIC DOMAIN RESOURCES

The following is a list of sources for photographs and illustrations for a variety of uses. This list was originally compiled by Wikipedia with the text descriptions edited for brevity. Collections that allow public contributions may or may not be monitored and depend on the care and knowledge of contributors to remain within the guidelines of the public domain laws.

Please carefully read each source's information on their images and any requirements/restrictions that may exist on use. Groups listed may have public domain or royalty-free images mixed with others still covered by copyrights. Inclusion in this list does not guarantee appropriateness for your specific project use.

- Wikimedia Commons - http://en.wikipedia.org/wiki/Wikipedia_commons - freely licensed images, sound files, and other media. 18 million+ files. Contains many public domain images. Commons is the primary repository of media for all Wikimedia projects. Media on Commons can be used readily on all Wikimedia projects, just as if the media were uploaded to the projects directly. Media tagged with the Creative Commons Public Domain Mark can be found here: commons:Category:CC-PD-Mark
- Pixabay – http://pixabay.com - 100,000 public domain photos and clipart images, under Creative Commons CC0 - free for private and commercial use.
- PublicPhoto.Org - Over 26,000 unique photos with a resolution of up to 4752 x 3168 px free for private and commercial use.
- PD Photo – http://pdphoto.org - Large collection of mostly public domain photos. Read the license for each picture before use; model releases have been obtained for all photos.
- Photos Public Domain – www.photos-public-domain.com - Thousands of high quality public domain photographs free for any use, with no restrictions. Collections included are: textures, animals, nature, and a variety of stock images for any use, including commercial.
- PDPics – www.pdpics.com - Public domain photo collection with about 6500 high resolution pictures up to 6000x4000. All images licensed under CC0 license.
- BestPhoto.us – http://bestphotos.us - about 2500 free photos in various categories.

- **Picdrome** – http://picdrome.com - growing Public Domain picture collection: no copyright, licensed under Creative Commons CC0 1.0 Public Domain Dedication.
- **Alegri Photos** – http://www.alegriphotos.com - Public domain and Creative Commons images
- **Public-Domain-Photos.com**
- **4 Free Photos** – www.4freephotos.com - Public domain images.
- **Public Domain Files** – www.publicdomainfiles.com - Public domain pictures and clip art.
- **PD Poster** – http://pdposters.weebly.com - Public domain posters
- **Ars Publik** – www.arspublik.com - A collection of public domain images from the web, for use in web and graphic design.
- **RepublicDomain.com** - free public domain photos and desktop wallpapers.
- **Phototeria.com** The site presents a large Collection of Public Domain images only. It's very easy to navigate Phototeria.com which benefits not so experienced users or young folks.
- **clker** – www.clkr.com - Easy to search public domain images, directly usable in openoffice.org
- **Open Domain** – http://opendomain.blogspot.com - public domain images from various sources in one-a-day blog format.
- **Free Photos** – www.freephotos.se - Small personal photographic collection dedicated to the public domain.
- **Public Domain Footage** – www.publicdomainfootage.com - Public domain archival stock footage and newsreels.
- **Open Galleries** http://opengalleries.org - A community source of free photography, hosting several galleries with photos from all over the world.
- **The Public Domain Review** – http://publicdomainreview.org - A Blog by the Open Knowledge Foundation to easily access public domain resources.
- **Freetems** – http://freetems.net - Public Domain images, graphics and more, free without registration.
- **Public Domain Pictures** – www.publicdomainpictures.net - A large collection of high quality pictures for free. Possibility to contact the authors for original files. (For some photo you have to be "premium membership" a.k.a. you have to pay!).
- **FreeStockPhotos.biz** A large collection of Public Domain, GNU, Creative Commons & custom licensed stock photos and clip art. (Beware, CC images are not necessarily in the public domain).
- **Good Free Photos** – www.goodfreephotos.com - All public domain pictures of mainly landscape but wildlife and plants as well
- **My Public Domain Pictures** – www.mypublicdomainpictures.com - A growing collection of amateur pictures released into public domain. You can use their pictures for any purpose and they do not require anything in return. Their collection includes travel pictures, pictures of animals and

plants, background designs and many more being added everyday. They also include a collection of high resolution public domain pictures segregated according to topics including etchings of public domain pictures. The site also includes macro photography.

Government resources

Google repository of LIFE images – http://images.google.com/hosted/life - hosts a large repository of LIFE images; Time Warner, Inc. claims blanket copyright to everything but this is simply untrue. (see here and also see here) Anything more than 120 years old (i.e., before 1892) is generally safe. (exception is if the original author died less than 75 years ago—45 years after these PD pictures have been taken—the author lived in a state with Common law copyright, and the name of the author is known—and in that case Time itself is most likely in copyright violation.) You *must* remove the watermark if you use the larger image.

- **TotallyFreeImages.com** - Totally free public-domain images - This is the largest archive on the Internet with more than 494,000 high-resolution, professional-grade, royalty-free images, 100% public-domain and acceptable for use with Wikipedia. (collection from government sources)
- **The Best Copyright-Free Photo Libraries** - http://www.dotgovwatch.com/?/archives/8-The-Best-Copyright-Free-Photo-Libraries.html- search for images on government sites
- **http://www.unclesamsphotos.com** a detailed directory of the U.S. government's public domain image galleries
- **USCITES.gov/imagegallery** - Endangered species photos, illustrations and video provided by the U.S. delegation to the Convention on International Trade in Endangered Species of Wild Fauna and Flora (CITES)
- **http://www.archive.org/details/USGovernmentDocuments** Government Documents scanned by the Internet Archive
- **U.S. National Park Service Historic Photograph Collection – www.nps.gov/hfc/cfm/npsphoto.cfm**
- **http://images.fws.gov/** - U.S. Fish and Wildlife Service imagery
- **images.google.com** - use the advanced search feature to return images from the site or domain ".gov". {{PD-USGov}} may apply to such images.
- **http://images.usace.army.mil/main.html** - United States Army Corps of Engineers Digital Visual Library
- **U.S. Library of Congress digital image archive** – http://memory.loc.gov - Some images are still under copyright, so be aware and read all notations carefully.

- **National Atlas** - http://nationalatlas.gov Lots of .GIF image maps, such as Congressional District maps, all in the public domain.
- **U.S. Department of Agriculture Natural Resources Conservation Service Photo Gallery** – http://photogallery.nrca.usda.give/res/sites/photogallery - Photo gallery for Department of Agriculture
- **U.S. Antarctic Program Photo Library** – http://photogallery.usap.gov
- http://terraserver-usa.com/default.aspx - free public access to a vast data store of maps and aerial photographs of the United States originating from USGS. {{PD-USGov-USGS}} may apply to such images.
- http://visualsonline.cancer.gov/ -Great resource for electron microscopy and histological images. Includes general biomedical and science-related images, cancer-specific scientific and patient care-related images, and portraits of directors and staff of the National Cancer Institute.
- USDA Agriculture Research Service Image gallery – http://ars.usda.gov/is/graphics/photos. A complimentary source of high-quality digital photographs available from the Agricultural Research Service Information Staff.
- **U.S. Census Bureau Photo Services** – www.census.gov/pubinfo/www/broadcast/photos - media "are free to use in news media and public information products" but are not in the public domain. Photo credit is requested, commercial use not allowed; see site for licence terms.
- http://www.defenselink.mil/multimedia/ - Current U.S. Department of Defense publicly released image
- http://www.defenseimagery.mil/ U.S. Department of Defense Visual Information Center (high-resolution U.S. military imagery; use with {{PD-USGov-Military-DVIC}} license template.)
- **The Congressional Pictorial Directory** – www.gpoaccess.gov/pictorial/index.html - also available in book form.
- Department of the Navy - Naval Historical Center Photographic Section – www.history.navy.mil/branches/nhcorg11.htm
- History of Medicine at the National Library of Medicine – www.nlm.nih.gov/hmd/index.html - Most but not all of the exhibitions are PD. Clicking on "Metadata" near the bottom of the page will generate a popup window with information that includes rights usage for each page.
- NOAA Photo Library – http://www.photolib.noaa.gov
- http://www.senate.gov and http://www.house.gov - Congressional sites have a broad variety of public domain images, especially photographs of representatives and senators.
- http://www.usa.gov/Topics/Graphics.shtml - A portal to U.S. government images and photos. "Most of these images and graphics are available for use in the public domain"

- USDA Online Photography Center - http://www.usda.gov/wps/portal/usda/usdahome?navtype=SU&navid= CSC_PHOTO_LIB
- Armed Forces Institute of Pathology – http://slides.afip.org Pathology and histology slides made by the U.S. government.
- MedPix Medical Image Database – **http://rad.usuhs.edu/medpix** - Hosting by Uniformed Services University of the Health Sciences. The terms of use of the site state that the original submitter may retain copyright. Nearly all of the submitters are U.S. government physicians. The status of the submitter is available to verify that an individual image is in the public domain.
- Uniformed Services University of the Health Sciences – www.usuhs.mil
- Oakland Public Library - **http://oac.cdlib.org/items/ark:/13030/kt5b69q5bc** - Not all are PD! The image detail page will state the status, PD images will be clearly marked "Public domain".
- http://srufaculty.sru.edu/david.dailey/public/public_domain.htm - Scanned and colorised etchings claimed to be PD images.
    If any page or image seems missing,
    replace http://www.sru.edu/depts/cisba/compsci/dailey *in*
    its URI with http://srufaculty.sru.edu/david.dailey/

- http://content.lib.washington.edu/costumehistweb/index.html - This collection includes 417 fashion plates from 1806-1914 from some of the leading fashion journals of the time.

Subject-based Collections

Ordered by subject, alphabetically:

Art

Note: Accurate photographs of two-dimensional visual artworks lack expressive content and are automatically in the public domain once the painting's copyright has expired (which it has in the US if it was published before 1923). All other copyright notices can safely be ignored.

- http://www.ibiblio.org/wm/paint/
- http://siris-artinventories.si.edu/ - The Smithsonian Institution Research Information System (SIRIS) is an American art catalog compiled by the Smithsonian Institute. It has many reproductions of

American paintings. However, it is known to have a number of factual errors, so it should be used with great care.

- http://www.artrenewal.org/pages/artistindex.php - Images of the works of more than 2,600 realist painters, many in the public domain; check catalogue for dates of works and artists. Note: Accurate photographs of two-dimensional visual artworks lack expressive content and are automatically in the public domain once the painting's copyright has expired (which it has in the US if it was published before 1923). All other copyright notices can safely be ignored.
- http://www.thefamousartists.com - Growing resource with biographies and selected works of artists whose works are all in the public domain.

Automotive

- The Crittenden Automotive Library. Search for it in http://www.Archive.org. Not all are PD! The image detail page will state the status, PD images will be marked "Public domain" or by year of publication if before 1922.

Clip Art

Clip art, in the graphic arts, refers to pre-made images used to illustrate any medium. Clip art is generally composed exclusively of illustrations (created by hand or by computer software), and does not include stock photography. That artwork may be in any number of digital formats.

- http://www.wpclipart.com - exists to maintain and grow an online collection of artwork for schoolkids and others that is free of copyright concerns as well as safe from inappropriate images. To ensure these qualities, no direct user-uploaded images are allowed. This is one of the largest collections of public domain images online (clip art and photos), and the fastest-loading. Maintainer vets all images and promptly answers email inquiries.
- Open Clip Art – http://www.openclipart.org. This project is an archive of public domain clip art. The clip art is stored in the W3C scalable vector graphics (SVG) format.
- http://www.incredibleart.org/links/clipart.html (a lengthy list of categorised links to other public domain image sources, many of those links don't work though)

- Public Domain Clip Art- 25,000+ Public Domain Clip Arts (good for printing). Categorized & searchable.
- Clip Art/Public Domain at the Open Directory Project (a list of links to sites with public domain clip art)

Computer-generated

- http://woodshole.er.usgs.gov/mapit/ - Automatic public domain map generating program
- http://www.collectionscanada.ca/cin/index-e.html - Canadian Illustrated News, 1869-1883
- PAT public domain country and regional maps

History

- http://ushistoryimages.com - Public domain images from United States history.
- http://www.acliparthistory.com - Public Domain images of the History of the World. Also Natural History and Fancy letters suitable for school projects
- http://lcweb2.loc.gov/ammem/ammemhome.html Library of Congress American Memory site (Check copyright information for the separate items before deciding to use them!)
- http://www.exclassics.com/newgate/ngillus.htm Images from The Newgate Calendar. Mostly crimes and criminals from the 18th century. Also other works athttp://www.exclassics.com
- http://www.fromoldbooks.org/ Collection images scanned from various old books that are now in the public domain. Searchable.
- http://www.john-leech-archive.org.uk/ John Leech sketch archives 1841 until 1864 from Punch magazine The page states they are long out of copyright and that they are believed to be public domain.
- http://beinecke.library.yale.edu/ Yale University's Beinecke Rare Book & Manuscript Library's online collection of digital images. Most will be {PD-art}. 90,000 images from rare books and manuscripts, search by keyword.
- http://digitalgallery.nypl.org New York Public Library. Over 700,000 images scanned from books. Including illuminated manuscripts, historical maps, vintage posters, rare prints and photographs, illustrated books, printed ephemera, and more. There is a per-image usage fee even for public domain images.
- http://www.oldbookillustrations.com/ Images scanned from old books. States that images on the site are the works of artists who

"...have been dead for over seventy years, which makes them part of the public domain in many countries". Searchable by keywords.

- America As It Was - a huge resource for vintage postcards in the U. S., organized by state. Any postcard first published in the U. S. before 1978 without an explicit copyright notice is PD. Lots of photos, aerial views, and maps of many U. S. locations.
- "The Secret Museum of Mankind" - collection of anthropological photographs published in a 1935 book without copyright. Scanned and released under a CC-NC license, but images should be public domain, at least in the US, since they are faithful reproductions of PD images. (Warning: strong 1930's racist P. O. V.)

Specific periods

- World War II Poster Collection – http://digital.library.northwestern.edu/wwii-posters - over 300 posters issued by U. S. Federal agencies
- Photos of the Great War – www.gwpda.org/photos/greatwar.htm - many images of World War I, scanned in from public domain resources. Slight usage notice, which is probably compatible with GFDL (requires attribution and link, as does GFDL, requests e-mail notice of usage).
- The Heritage of the Great War – http://greatwar.nl/kleur/kleur.html - has several color pictures from World War I (likely all PD)
- World's Armed Forces Forum - http://www.network54.com/Forum/211833/thread/1088370788/last-1088%20381193/Colour+WWI+photos+%28must+see%21%21%29 (gallery for images taken from the French Ministry of Culture's website – www.culture.gouv.fr) hosts more colour images of World War I (likely all PD, since the effort taken to scan/reproduce them probably fails to qualify for being a derivative work).
- http://www.historyplace.com/unitedstates/childlabor/ Child Labor in America 1908 - 1912 by Lewis W. Hine
- Franklin D. Roosevelt Presidential Library and Museum - http://www.fdrlibrary.marist.edu/archives/collections/photographs.html - Thousands of on-line, copyright free photographs of Franklin and Eleanor Roosevelt, The Great Depression and the New Deal, and World War II.

Literature

- http://archive.org - Scanned-in books, maps, manuscripts, and historical documents; Public Domain; available in a number of formats including epub, kindle, and daisy; Searchable. This is an unbelievably large resource.

- http://openlibrary.org - Project of the Internet Archive to provide a web page for every book.
- http://books.google.com - Scanned-in books & historical documents. Keyword searchable. Great source for diagrams/illustrations. (not all public domain, many still in copyright) Books google believes are in the public domain are available for download as pdf.
- http://gutenberg.org - Scanned-in books. Searchable.
- http://catalog.hathitrust.org - Scanned-in books from partner universities. Searchable.

Logos and flags

- http://www.wpclipart.com/flags/index.html 436 flags, countries listed alphabetically, also US State flags, historical and others. All in PNG format.
- http://www.openclipart.org/
- https://www.cia.gov/library/publications/the-world-factbook/index.html CIA World Factbook

Mexico

- PlayaDelCarmenMexico.org Public domain photos of Playa del Carmen.

Music

- FreePD.com - sells original public domain music
- The Mutopia Project – www.ibiblio.org/mutopia - (not only) public domain sheet music

New Zealand

- Free New Zealand Photos – www.freenzphotos.com -Free photos of New Zealand under Creative Common license.

Religion

- http://www.theworkofgodschildren.org Collection of high-resolution images of the Roman Catholic saints, religious symbols and related imagery. All pictures have been released into the public domain.
- http://www.coolnotions.com/PDImages/pd_StoryOfTheBible.htm Collection of Public Domain pictures from the Bible.

United States

Florida

- Florida Memory Project - http://www.floridamemory.com/photographiccollection/Contains Public Domain images taken in Florida.
- State of Florida Library - http://dlis.dos.state.fl.us/library/collections.cfm - Contains photographs and documents dealing with Florida.

APPENDIX B – GROUP MANAGEMENT FORMS

Why recreate the tracking forms contained within the book when you can download them? With online access and Microsoft Excel, you can download the forms. Access the Excel spreadsheet by emailing author GaryZenker@gmail.com and requesting it.

APPENDIX C - MEETUP REFERENCE SITES

To review some of the example sites mentioned within this book:

Main Line Writers Group
http://www.meetup.com/Main-Line-Writers/
www.MainLineWritersGroup.com

Wilmington Writers Group
http://www.meetup.com/Wilmington-Writers-Group/
www.WilmingtonWritersGroup.com

Brandywine Valley Writers Group
http://www.meetup.com/Brandywine-Valley-Writers-Group/

ABOUT THE AUTHOR

Gary Zenker is a marketing professional with over 25 years of experience in creating Business and Marketing Plans, and managing marketing implementations. His work includes collateral creation, web site design and content, advertising optimization and social media. He has a shelf full of awards recognizing his work in  multiple industries but is most proud of the millions of dollars he has generated in sales and cost savings for his clients.

In his various positions, Gary has been responsible for a variety of meetings and events, including annual shareholder meetings and events, national trade shows, convention coordination and attendance, non-profit event coordination, sales meetings, volunteer coordination, and other related event coordination.

Gary currently leads The Main Line Writers Group, founded in 2009, and the Wilmington Writers Group, founded in 2013, dedicated to helping writers of all experience levels and genres better their craft. He also ran Maketing Majik, a marketing Meetup for entrepreneurs and served the Brandywine Valley Writers Group in a leadership role, as well.

He is also the owner of White Lightning Publications which has published a total of eleven books to date. Gary lives in West Chester, Pennsylvania. He and his son Seth have co-authored two books – *Says Seth* and the forthcoming *Deathfarts.com: More Says Seth* which he observes "will make you laugh heartily and shoot whatever you are drinking through your nose." He recommends you swallow your drink before reading these books.

ACKNOWLEDGEMENTS

This book is the result of a suggestion from Main Line Writers Group member and cartoonist Brian Mahon. Thank you, Brian, for being so impressed with the group itself and offering up the idea. I hope that the book offers all that it should to those who read it.

The leadership skills used in the groups and presented in the book are the result of working for and with hundreds of very talented business people throughout my career who taught everyone around them by example. I can't possibly name them all individually but I recognize you, here, in the aggregate.

In creating this book, three members of the Main Line Writers were kind enough to volunteer to review the entire book in detail. It was a big job! There's no way to appropriately express my gratitude for the many hours and huge effort they placed into helping me create a better book...but I should really try.

Judy Di Canio offered a detailed review of the book and many suggestions to make it stronger. She also offered encouraging words about the entire effort and my writing style itself. It shouldn't be a surprise as she teaches writing and offers professional consulting and encouragement to many writers.

Gerri Lambert poured over the entire text in detail and then in addition spent hours reviewing them with me to help to make it better. At the same time, she made lots of general suggestions that she felt would benefit the group itself...and they have.

Susanna Reilly was the first to offer to review the book and offered insights and comments, proofread and helped me create the publishable, finished draft of the book. As she plays a significant role in the group itself, I am very happy to have her insights represented.

All three reviewers also helped change negative references into positive ones. I am grateful to all of you for your hard work and even more so for your friendship!

I reference my own Meetup groups throughout this book and leadership is such an important component of managing them. There are many people within our groups that are part of that leadership who help make those groups successful and they deserve to be recognized. Each of those mentioned is also awesome writer in his or her own right, breaking the stereotype of introvert writers. Any mention of leading the Main Line Writers Group without also mentioning their names would be leaving out a critical element of its success. I am immensely grateful to them for their participation in and dedication to the group.

Tony Conaway has a presence and voice that nobody forgets. He started the Main Line Writers Group with me and participates actively in nearly every group that I do. He is one of the most sharing writing professionals I have ever met. Everybody who runs a group needs their own Tony. Sorry, you can't have mine.

Susanna Reilly has been with the Main Line Writers Group from the beginning, serves as the group Treasurer and is the person who makes it easy for me not to obsess on membership fees. She is also my first go-to for honest opinions on my own performance as a leader and guidance in all things related to the group. You can't have her, either.

Paul Popeil has also been with the Main Line Writers Group since the beginning and guides all things Critique related. He not only runs critique during the regular meetings but also holds and runs special sessions for the members. He generously shares his talent and skills with the group and they are better for it.

Walter Lawn became the project manager for the story collection that the group produced and showed leadership as he gently *shoved us* toward structure and organization for the project. He is also my favorite poet with his mastery of words.

Liz Stollar took on and managed the Main Line Writers Group book launch, making it one of the most successful events I have seen. So besides being a damn talented writer, she is also a remarkable event planner.

And to all of the members of all of the groups who let me play leader, I thank you. You are the most talented collection of individuals I have ever met. It is an honor to provide you with a home and a structure to learn, grow and share.

75344679R00104

Made in the USA
Columbia, SC
20 August 2017